PASSIVE INCOME

How you can create a Multi-level empire that you can leave for your family

Jack Bennett

Table of Contents

CHAPTER 1:
WHAT DO SUCCESSFUL BUSINESS PEOPLE DO

Lots of people have the dream, but they get bogged down in the details of how to go about it. This book is meant to serve as a complete business guide; it will give you an idea of some of the steps involved in owning your business.

Hire Professionals

The most important professionals you'll need at the beginning are a lawyer and an accountant. The lawyer can help you decide if you want to be a corporation, partnership, sole proprietorship, or some other type of company. A good accountant can help you make this decision based on which will be most advantageous to you from a tax angle. A lawyer can also help you register your business and get any licenses and permits you will need, and can advise you about patenting your idea or protecting your intellectual property by requiring everyone you discuss your business with to sign non-disclosure or confidentiality agreements.

Make a Business Plan

You may need to hire a writer or other business professional to help you write a business plan. You'll need one to help yourself get organized as to what your business's main purpose or goal will be. This could be anything from serving hot dogs to people outside the home improvement store to providing technology support to major players in the business world. Either way, you need a plan that sketches out how you will proceed toward your goal and an estimate of how much money you'll need to get there. What will your equipment costs be? Will you be hiring employees? How about renting office space? All of these cost estimates should be included in your Business Plan.

Get Financing

How much start-up money will you need? Do you have savings you can use? Friends or business associates who might want to invest in your venture? Or do you need a bank loan? Whatever the situation, you'll need to present a copy of your business plan to bankers or investors if you need to borrow money to get your company rolling.

Set Up Your Record-keeping System

A good accountant can advise you on the best record-keeping software for your business, and help you set up a system for keeping track of payables, receivables, sales tax, payroll, employee benefits plans, and so forth. You will be relying on the accountant for at least your yearly tax return for your business, and possibly for quarterly payroll and sales tax returns. Your accountant can also get you an EIN number (Employer Identification Number).

Find a Location

Depending on your business, location may be very important. If you need to be visible to the public (say your business is a bookstore or restaurant), then you'll have to think long and hard about where you should set up shop. Location can make you or break you-and the rent is due no matter which way your fortune turns. You will also need to get a phone, get the utilities turned on, install your furniture and equipment, and get a sign or two that shouts "Hey look! We're here!"

Set Up Accounts with Credit Card Companies

Every brick-and-mortar business these days takes plastic or they don't stay in business. You'll pay a small percentage for every credit or debit card transaction a customer makes. You will need to invest in a method for checking the validity of debit and credit cards-like those "Slide Card Here" machines at cash registers everywhere.

Hire Employees

You may not need to do this step if you're a one-person operation. Maybe you can get by with just one part-time person to answer phones and do some of the paperwork. Of course, it depends on your business. You can probably run a small bookstore by yourself, but even a tiny restaurant means you'll need a cook, several servers, someone at the cashier, and so forth. You'll need to have them complete various forms for the IRS, and you may want to run background checks or at least check some references before you hire anyone.

Promote Your Business

Decide how you will let people know you exist, what you can do for them, and why they should come to you instead of someone else. Common forms of advertising are TV and radio commercials, newspaper ads, flyers, and coupons that appear in booklets distributed by local companies. The list might make you think twice about starting a business of your own. Perhaps you aren't looking to make such a financial commitment regarding the hiring of professionals, finding a location. There is a very simple way of attaining this goal that has worked well for millions of people. You can have your very own business in your home, and you can cross off all or most of the steps listed above. The best part of exploring home-based business opportunities is that there is little risk and the upside is tremendous. Many of the inconveniences and pressures of the traditional business are wiped away with the home business. The biggest roadblock to starting or buying a business is that they require a considerable up-front cash investment. In addition to the large investment, the time commitment you must make when starting a business can ultimately turn out to be far greater than what you have experienced in any job, and the return is not necessarily worth the extra time or the financial risk.

SUCCESSFUL BUSINESS PEOPLE

Dan Kennedy

People often wonder exactly how Dan Kennedy has helped transform so many businesses into million-dollar income producers. Not to mention how many businesses he's sparked income improvement in. Especially when you look at the wide and diverse range of product and service categories he's worked with...everything from professional practices such as doctors, dentists, financial advisors and chiropractors to auto repair shops, retail stores and restaurants to info-products, authors, consultants and coaches.

Why do they wonder?

They usually want to know how they can have the same kind of success in their business. Well, the one thing Dan Kennedy attributes most of his success to his ability to write persuasive, compelling copy. And while I agree, I also contend that there is another simple thing Dan does that has greatly impacted the level of his success. It's something that anyone can do. But, shockingly...only a very tiny percentage of the population actually does it. In fact, even after reading this, you'd be surprised at how many people won't follow this simple advice. The proof

I have that this one simple thing is a big part of Dan's success formula is that the most successful people I know all do this. And, Dan teaches that this is critical to get things "right." In fact, if you want to be successful, I believe you could greatly accelerate the process by following Dan's example.

What is it that Dan and the upper echelon do that most don't?

Sure as an author, coach, consultant, and speaker Dan gets paid to talk and give advice. His written words have earned him millions of dollars and his advice has created over a billion dollars in revenue for those who have followed it. However, before Dan dispenses advice to a client, GKIC member, or coaching group, he asks questions... And then he shuts up and focuses all his attention on listening. In fact, he won't utter a word of advice until after he's asked questions. He also has a long history of seeking out the biggest achievers. Dan surrounds himself with them and always has—even in his earliest days. In the midst of these achievers he's always asking questions, listening and taking notes. You'll find when you meet him during our big events such as Super Conference℠ and Info-SUMMIT℠ that he doesn't talk much. You might even describe him as quiet or reserved because he doesn't go on about how great he is or how he's accomplished this or that—which he most certainly could do. Instead he tends to listen. Sure, he offers advice, but only when asked. Those who have meet with Dan knows that he doesn't barrel in with advice...instead he leads with a question about our results, approach, target audience, goals, etc. Such a simple formula, yet so many don't utilize it. I believe this is due to a couple of reasons.

One, I think people are embarrassed. Somehow we've been taught to believe that not knowing the answer to something or asking a question that in our minds isn't "good enough" will make a negative impression. Of course, now that you know that the smartest people ask questions, this should no longer apply. But if you are still feeling that way, then asking your question one on one rather than in front of a large group might help your anxiety or embarrassment. Another reason is that sometimes people feel uncertain about what to ask. While you will get better at this with practice, you might have a list of go-to questions you use. For example, you've probably heard Dan say that the wealthiest, most successful people he meets are always asking people what books they are reading. Before attending a convention, networking or other big event, take the time to jot down three of the biggest challenges you are facing in your business or life. Then frame your questions around these.

For example, let's say you own a brick and mortar retail store and your number one goal is to raise the amount of your average transaction. When you attend Super Conference^{SM} you might ask everyone you meet what they are doing to increase transaction amounts with their customers. When you do this, you are bound to find ideas that will work in your business too. Or perhaps there is something specific you want to learn how to do such as mobile marketing or purchase direct mail lists. You could ask people if they've had a successful experience using mobile marketing. If they say yes, then ask if they have advice for someone starting out about what to do or what not to do. By having a pre-defined list of what you want to know about, you'll find it much easier to ask questions and get answers to your most pressing concerns. While you can learn from anyone, you'll excel the fastest by seeking out and asking questions to the most successful people in the room. And you'll be a better author, coach, consultant, info-marketer, retailer, professional, etc. when you seek to understand and clarify your client or customer's problem first through questions before you diagnosis or dispense advice.

Richard Branson

I am often asked if I have found a secret or at least a consistent answer to successfully building businesses over my career. So I've spent some time thinking about what characterizes so many of Virgin's successful ventures and, importantly, what went wrong when we did not get it right. Reflecting across 40 years I have come up with five "secrets."

No1: Enjoy what you are doing:

Because starting a business is a huge amount of hard work, requiring a great deal of time, you had better enjoy it. When I started Virgin from a basement flat in West London, I did not set out to build a business empire. I set out to create something I enjoyed that would pay the bills.

There was no great plan or strategy: The name itself was thought up on the hoof. One night some friends and I were chatting over a few drinks and decided to call our group Virgin, as we were all new to business. The name stuck and had a certain ring to it. For me, building a business is all about doing something to be proud of, bringing talented people together and creating something that's going to make a real difference to other people's lives.

A businesswoman or a businessman is not unlike an artist: What you have when you start a company is a blank canvas; you have to fill it. Just as a good artist has to get every single detail right on that canvas, a businessman or businesswoman has to get every single little thing right when first setting up in business in order to succeed. However, unlike a work of art, the business is never finished. It constantly evolves. If a businessperson sets out to make a real difference to other people's lives, and achieves that, he or she will be able to pay the bills and have a successful business to boot.

No. 2: Create something that stands out.

Whether you have a product, a service or a brand, it is not easy to start a company and to survive and thrive in the modern world. In fact, you've got to do something radically different to make a mark today. Look at the most successful businesses of the past 20 years. Microsoft, Google or Apple, for example, shook up a sector by doing something that hadn't ever been done and by continually innovating. They are now among the dominant forces.

No. 3: Create something that everybody who works for you is really proud of

Businesses generally consist of a group of people, and they are your biggest assets.

No. 4: Be a good leader

As a leader you have to be a really good listener. You need to know your own mind but there is no point in imposing your views on others without some debate. No one has a monopoly on good ideas or good advice. Get out there, listen to people, draw people out and learn from them. As a leader you've also got to be extremely good at praising people. Never openly criticize people; never lose your temper, and always lavish praise on your colleagues for a job well done.

People flourish if they're praised: Usually they don't need to be told when they've done wrong because most of the time they know it. If somebody is not working out, don't automatically throw him or her out of the company. A company should genuinely be a family. So see if there's another job within the company that suits them better. On most occasions you'll find something for every single kind of personality.

No. 5: Be Visible

A good leader does not get stuck behind a desk. I've never worked in an office – I've always worked from home – but I get out and about, meeting people. It seems I am traveling all the time but I always have a notebook in my back pocket to jot down questions, concerns or good ideas.

If I'm on a Virgin Atlantic plane, I make certain to get out and meet all the staff and many of the passengers. If you meet a group of Virgin Atlantic crew members, you are going to have at least 10 suggestions or ideas. If I don't write them down, I may remember only one the next day. By writing them down, I remember all 10. Get out and shake hands with all the passengers on the plane, and again, there are going to be people who had a problem or have a suggestion. Write it down, make sure that you get their names, get their e-mail addresses, and make sure the next day that you respond to them. Of course, I try to make sure that we appoint managing directors who have the same philosophy. That way we can run a large group of companies in the same way a small business owner runs a family business – keeping it responsive and friendly. When you're building a business from scratch, the key word for many years is "survival." It's tough to survive. In the beginning you haven't got the time or energy to worry about saving the world. You've just got to fight to make sure you can look after your bank manager and be able to pay the bills. Literally, your full concentration has to be on surviving. Obviously, if you don't survive, just remember that most businesses fail and the best lessons are usually learned from failure. You must not get too dispirited. Just get back up and try again.

BASIC RULES OF A SUCCESSFUL BUSINESS

What does it take to start and succeed in business? : Although there is no one answer that fits all businesses, there are a number of practices followed by successful business owners. No matter what you sell, you'll be ahead of the game if you live by these ten essential rules for succeeding in your own business.

1. ***Be true to yourself:*** No matter how much money someone else makes, if you don't enjoy the business, wouldn't be proud to show your relatives what you are doing and how you are doing it, then don't do it. If you run a business you don't like or don't believe in, even if you have temporary success, it will come back to haunt you one way or another.

2. ***Find a need and fill it:*** Yes, you've heard that a million times. But it still works. The easiest business to run is one that produces

products or services that people already know they need. The reason: you don't have to spend a lot of time and money convincing prospects they need what you sell. You can focus on why you are the best source to satisfy their need. Just be sure the "need" is one people will spend money to satisfy.

3. ***Choose products or services that you can sell for a lot more than it costs you to make or buy them:*** If the difference between your cost and selling prices is too low, you will have difficulty growing the business. When profit margins are too low, you won't have enough money to hire employees, pay for rent (when you need to move the business out of the house), advertise more, and do other things needed to expand.

4. ***Make realistic estimates of your expenses... then double them****:* Most new businesses either forget about marketing, fulfillment, overhead costs, income taxes and self-employment or greatly underestimate them.

5. ***Be true to your customers and prospects.*** Don't promise what you can't deliver. Don't lie or exaggerate the benefits of what you sell and always deliver a quality product or service. Word-of-mouth marketing

has always been one of the primary ways small businesses find customers. The Internet and social networking sites spread the word (good or bad) to even more potential customers.

6. ***Understand the importance of marketing and learn how to do it effectively.*** The world won't beat a path to your door just because you build a better mousetrap or write a great ebook about how to grow tomatoes or teach a child to read. To get customers you will have to market your products or services effectively and continually.

7. ***Treat your vendors, manufacturers and service providers with respect and let them know you appreciate them.*** They are an important part of your team and your success. If you speak down to them, pester them with questions you could answer yourself, imply that they don't' do a good job, nickel and dime them to death, or are an ongoing pain in the neck, they'll never go out of their way to help you -- and might drop you all together. No business needs picky, annoying, time-consuming customers.

8. ***Embrace the web.*** No matter what you sell or to whom, your customers will always turn to the web to research and/or buy. They may turn to online yellow pages to find a florist in Florence, SC; use voice recognition on their smart phone to find a nearby restaurant, or use their computer to go to Google, MSN or Yahoo to search for a phrase like "Elder law attorney Farmington Hills MI", or "plumber weekends Astoria NY." If customers can't find you in their queries, they are likely to give their business to one of your competitors.

9. ***Don't expect miracles.*** Yes, people do make money in their sleep or while they're away on vacation - the Internet makes that possible. But only after they've invested a lot of time, effort, and money in building the business and building the team that keeps it going and growing.

10. **Remind yourself that one is the loneliest number in business**. One product, one service, one main client, and all your records stored on one computer hard drive without regular off-site backups is a recipe for failure. If you only have one product or service you're missing out on the chance to profit by selling more things to people who already know and trust you. If you have only one main client, you're up the proverbial creek if they decide to change vendors or run into cash flow problems. And if all your records are on your computer and

you don't have always up-to-date backups of your important files, a hard drive crash could destroy your business.

GETTING YOUR BUSINESS PLAN SET

People are always asking for a list of fundamentals, a checklist they can use to start their own businesses. From your business type to your business model to your physical location, there are so many variables it's not easy to come up with a list that will work for everybody. The key, regardless of what type of business you're starting, is to be flexible!

1. Personal evaluation: Sabrina Parsons once said know yourself, and work in a job that caters to your strengths. This knowledge will make you happier. Begin by taking stock of yourself and your situation. Why do you want to start a business? Is it money, freedom, creativity, or some other reason? What skills do you have? What industries do you know about? Would you want to provide a service or a product? What do you like to do? How much capital do you have to risk? Will it be a full-time or a part-time venture? Your answers to these types of questions will help you narrow your focus. This step is not supposed to dissuade you from starting your own business. Rather, it's here to get you thinking and planning. In order to start a successful business, passion alone isn't enough. You need to plan, set goals and above all, know yourself. What are your strengths? What are your weaknesses? How will these affect day-to-day operations?

It's even better if you can enter a market you like and that you know well. As you get started, your business will likely dominate your life so make sure that what you're doing is stimulating and not dull. You're going to be in it for the long-haul. Some good questions to ask include:

What would you do if money wasn't the problem? Is money really important? Or rather, is making a lot of it really important? If it is, you're probably going to be cutting out a number of options.

What things really matter to you? Do you have the support of your family, especially your immediate family? They may have to make sacrifices at the beginning, so it's important to have them behind you.

Who do you admire in business? Perhaps in the industry you'd like to go into. Why do you admire them? What are their likable traits? What can you learn from them?

Answering these questions and asking many more about yourself and your abilities isn't necessarily going to ensure you're successful but it will get you thinking about your goals and about what motivates and inspires you. Use this time to make sure that you are matching the business you want to start to your personal aspirations.

2. Analyze the industry: Tim Berry said that the more you know about your industry, the more advantage and protection you will have. Once you decide on a business that fits your goals and lifestyle, you need to evaluate your idea. Who will buy your product or service? Who would be your competitors? You also need to figure out at this stage how much money you will need to get started. Your 'personal evaluation' was as much a reality check as a prompt to get you thinking. The same thing applies when it comes to researching your business and the industry you'd like to go into. There are a number of ways you can do this including performing general Google searches, going out and speaking to people already working in that industry, reading books by people from the industry, researching key people, reading relevant news sites and industry magazines and taking a class or two (if this is possible). If you don't have time to perform the research or would like a second opinion, there are people you can go to for help – government departments and your local Small Business Association.

Evaluating your market: In order to identify how attractive your prospective market really is (your own desires aside for the moment), there are a few things you should consider: How urgently do people need the thing you're selling/offering right now? What's the market size like? Are there already a lot of people paying for this thing? For example, the demand for 'traditional signwriting classes' is almost non-existent. How easy (and how much will it cost) to acquire a customer? If you're a lead generation business, this may require a significantly larger investment that say a coffee shop.

3. Make it legal: Realistically speaking, registering your business as a business is the first step toward making it real. However, as with the personal evaluation, take your time to get to know the pros and cons of different business formations.

Types of business formations includes; Sole proprietorship, Partnership, Corporation, Limited Liability Company (LLC). Spend some time getting to know the pros and cons of each business formation. If you need help, we've got a full guide on Legal Entities, Licenses and Permits. Other things you will need to do include deciding on a business name and researching availability for that name.

4. *Start the planning process:* Pablo Picasso said that our goals can only be reached through the vehicle of a plan, in which we must fervently believe, and upon which we must vigorously act and there is no other route to success. If you will be seeking outside financing, a business plan is a necessity. But, even if you are going to finance the venture yourself, a business plan will help you figure out how much money you will need in order to get started; what needs to get done when, and where you are headed. In the simplest terms, a business plan is a roadmap – something you will use to help you chart your progress and that will outline the things you need to do in order to achieve your goals. Rather than thinking of a business plan as a hefty document that you'll only use once (perhaps to obtain a loan from a bank), think of it as a way to formalize your intentions. While you will potentially use your business plan as part of your pitch to investors and banks, or use it to attract potential partners and board members, you will primarily use it to define your strategy, tactics and specific activities for execution, including key dates, deadlines and budgets, and cash flow. In fact, the business plan does not have to be a formal document at all if you don't need to present your plan to outsiders. Instead, your plan can follow a lean planning process that involves creating a pitch, forecasting your key business numbers, outlining key milestones you hope to achieve, and regular progress checks where you review and revise your plan. If you aren't presenting to investors, your pitch is not the traditional pitch presentation, but instead a high-level overview of who you are, the problem you are solving, your solution to the problem, your target market, and the key tactics you will use to achieve your goals. Even if you do not think you need a business plan, you should go through the planning process anyway. The process of doing so will help to uncover any holes or areas that have you have not thought through well enough. If you do need to write a formal business plan document, you should follow the outline below.

The standard business plan comprises nine parts, including:

- The Executive Summary

- Company Overview

- Products and Services

- Target Market

- Marketing and Sales Plan

- Milestones and Metrics

- Management Team

- Financial Plan

- Appendix

Types of Business Plans

If you are simply creating a business plan in order to stimulate a discussion with potential partners and associates, you may want to consider opting for a 'startup plan', also known as a feasibility plan. As your business grows you can flesh out the sections as you see fit. In contrast to the standard plan and the startup plan, is the operation or annual plan. This type of plan is used for internal purposes and primarily reflects the needs of the members of the company. This type of plan is not intended for banks and outside investors. You will use it either to plan your company's growth or expansion, or to set company-wide priorities. If the latter is true and you are using the plan in order to direct your internal strategy, you are creating a strategic plan, a type of plan that will include a high-level strategy, tactical foundations of the strategy, specific responsibilities, activities, deadlines and budgets, and a financial plan.

5. Get financed: Depending on the size of your venture, you may need to seek financing from an angel or from a venture capital firm. Most small businesses begin with private financing from credit cards, personal loans, help from the family, etc. As a rule of thumb, besides your start-up costs, you should also have at least three months' worth of your family's budget in the bank. In order to finance your company, you will need to match the company's needs to the appropriate financing option. The main types of investment and lending options include:

- Venture capital

- Angel investment (similar to venture capital)

- Commercial (banks)

- The Small Business Administration (SBA)

- Accounts receivable specialists

- • Friends and family

Note: a beautifully fleshed-out business plan does not guarantee you will get funded. In fact, according to Guy Kawasaki, the business plan is one of the least influential factors when it comes to raising money: To stand a realistic chance of getting hold of the funds that you need before you can get started, you'd be better off first focusing on your 'pitch'. Not only will it be easier to fix because it contains less, but you'll also get feedback on it – most investors don't bother reading the full business plan, though they may still expect you to have it. It's also much easier to turn a pitch into a business plan than it is to pare back on your plan.

6. Set up shop: You've done it. Or just about. Your business plan has been laid out, the money is in the bank and you're raring to go. You've got a long list of things you need to do:

Find a location. Negotiate leases. Buy inventory. Get the phones installed. Have stationery printed. Hire staff. Set your prices. Throw a "Grand Opening" party. Each of these steps will need to be thought through carefully.

How to setup a shop; Your business location will dictate the type of customer you attract, what types of promotions you can run and how long it will take you to grow. While a great location won't necessarily guarantee your success, a bad location will almost always guarantee failure. As you're thinking about where you want to set up shop (including the city and state), consider the following:

Price – can you realistically afford to be where you want to be? If not, or if you're cutting it fine, keep looking.

Visibility – will people easily be able to find you? Will they see your promotions and offers? Are you in the center of town or further out? How will this affect you?

Access to parking or public transportation – can people easily find you? If they have to look too hard, they may give up.

Distribution of competitors – are there many competitors close to you? If so, this may be a sign that the location is Premium for the clientele you wish to attract. It may also mean you do no business. Consider carefully how you wish to approach this type of situation.

Local, city and state rules and regulations – some may be more stringent than others. Ensure there are no restrictions that will limit your operations or that will act as barriers to your store.

7. Trial and error: Whether you're starting your first or your third business, expect to make mistakes. This is natural and as long as you learn from them, also beneficial. If you do not make mistakes, you do not learn what to do less of or equally, what to do more of, be open-minded and creative, adapt and look for opportunities and above all, have fun!

CHAPTER 2:
ANALYZE THE DIFFERENCE BETWEEN LLC CORPORATION AND SOLE PROPIETORSHIP

A limited liability company is a unique business entity that allows the company to have the same limited liability protection as a corporation, and the operational flexibility that a partnership has. On the other hand, sole proprietorships are the easiest and most cost effective type of business to form and operate.

Liability

Perhaps the biggest difference between a sole proprietorship and an LLC is the issue of limited liability protection. Sole proprietors have unlimited liability for business debts, lawsuits and other business-related obligations. This means sole proprietors are held personally liable for all debts incurred while operating the business. If the assets of a sole proprietorship are not enough to meet the company's debts, creditors may go after a sole proprietor's personal assets to satisfy the obligation. Operating as an LLC provides the owners of the company with limited liability protection against company debts and obligations. Creditors and parties that initiate a lawsuit against an LLC cannot go after an owner's personal assets as compensation for business-related debts.

Control

Sole proprietors have full control over the business, including how the company uses its proceeds. In a sole proprietorship, there are no other businesses or individuals to share business ideas with. The sole proprietor alone will have to make every decision regarding how to operate the company, and use the company's resources. LLCs with more than one owner have other members and managers to provide input regarding how to manage the business. In addition, owners of an LLC can choose to hire outside individuals to manage the company, as opposed to handling the company's day-to-day affairs.

Raising Money

Sole proprietorships have more difficulty raising money than an LLC. For starters, a sole proprietorship may be viewed as having less credibility, since the business owner did not take the time or pay the expense to incorporate or form an LLC. Lack of credibility makes it harder for a sole proprietorship to get loans, and could force the business owner to rely on business assets and personal credit history to raise funds for the business. LLCs may offer ownership interest in the business in exchange for money which will help finance the company's expansion. When a sole proprietor offers ownership in the business to another business or person, the company will no longer be treated as a sole proprietorship.

Ownership

A business can have only one person acting as the company's owner in order to earn treatment as a sole proprietorship. Another business, trust or estate may not participate in ownership of a sole proprietorship. Conversely, an LLC may have an unlimited number of owners that may consist of foreign businesses, corporations, other LLCs and partnerships.

Existence

An LLC may exist forever, regardless of who the manager or members of the company are. A sole proprietorship will cease to exist when a business owner dies, retires or decides to sell the business. LLCs may have an operating agreement that indicates provisions for continuing the company in the event of a member's death, withdrawal or retirement.

LIMITED PARTNERSHIP

A limited partnership is a form of partnership similar to a general partnership; except that where a general partnership must have at least two general partners (GPs) a limited partnership must have at least one GP and at least one limited partner. The GPs are, in all major respects, in the same legal position as partners in a conventional firm, i.e. they have management control, share the right to use partnership property, share the profits of the firm in predefined proportions, and have joint and several liabilities for the debts of the partnership. As in a general partnership, the GPs have actual authority, as agents of the firm, to bind the partnership in contracts with third parties that are in the ordinary course of the partnership's business. As with a general partnership, "an act of a general partner which is not apparently for carrying on in the ordinary course the limited partnership's activities or activities of the kind carried on by the limited partnership binds the limited partnership only if the act was actually authorized by all the other partners.

Like shareholders in a corporation, limited partners have limited liability. This means that the limited partners have no management authority, and (unless they obligate themselves by a separate contract such as a guaranty) are not liable for the debts of the partnership. The limited partnership provides the limited partners a return on their investment (similar to a dividend), the nature and extent of which is usually defined in the partnership agreement. General Partners thus bear more economic risk than do limited partners, and in cases of financial loss, the GPs will be the ones which are personally liable. Limited partners are subject to the same alter-ego piercing theories as corporate shareholders. However, it is more difficult to pierce the limited partnership veil because limited partnerships do not have a great many formalities to maintain. So long as the partnership and the members do not co-mingle funds, it would be difficult to pierce the veil. Limited partners are sometimes referred to as "silent partners" - in other words, they can make investments in the company but have no voting power or control over its day-to-day operations. They can be a valuable source of capital in this business structure. Limited partnership is the entity of choice for many law, accounting and finance firms. It's also a popular among businesses that focus on time-restricted projects, such as real estate and film production companies.

Advantages of a limited partnership include:

Personal asset protection: The limited partnership structure offers liability protection up to the amount of the investment for the company's limited partners.

Pass-through taxation: A limited partnership's income is not taxed at the business level; instead, business profit and loss are "passed through" to the partners for reporting on their personal tax returns.

Full oversight: The general partner has complete management control of the limited partnership.

Investment potential: Limited partnerships can generate capital investments by adding more limited partners.

Partnership interests are afforded a significant level of protection through the charging order mechanism. The charging order limits the creditor of a debtor-partner or a debtor-member to the debtor's share of distributions, without conferring on the creditor any voting or management rights. When the partnership is being constituted, or the composition of the firm is changing, limited partnerships are generally required to file documents with the relevant state registration office. Limited partners must explicitly disclose their status when dealing with other parties, so that such parties are on notice that the individual negotiating with them carries limited liability. It is customary that the notepaper, other documentation, and electronic materials issued to the public by the firm will carry a clear statement identifying the legal nature of the firm and listing the partners separately as general and limited. Hence, unlike the GPs, the limited partners do not have inherent agency authority to bind the firm unless they are subsequently held out as agents (and so create an agency by estoppels); or acts of ratification by the firm create ostensible authority. Limited partnerships are distinct from limited liability partnerships, in which all partners have limited liability. In some jurisdictions, the limited liability of the limited partners is contingent on their not participating in management.

In the United States, the limited partnership organization is most common among film production companies and real estate investment projects, or in types of businesses that focus on a single or limited-term project. They are also useful in "labor-capital" partnerships, where one or more financial backers prefer to contribute money or resources while the other partner performs the actual work. In such situations, liability is the driving concern behind the choice of limited partnership status. The limited partnership is also attractive to firms wishing to provide shares to many individuals without the additional tax liability of a corporation. Private equity companies almost exclusively use a combination of general and limited partners for their investment funds. Well-known limited partnerships include Enterprise Products and Blackstone Group (both of which are public companies), and Bloomberg L.P. (a private company).

THE DIFFERENCE BETWEEN CREATING SUSTAINABLE INCOME AND PASSIVE INCOME

Sustainable Income

Sustainable income is the most likely level of income to be obtained in the future. The desire to establish sustainable income is why we have a multi-step income statement. The most likely sustainable income is Income from Operations (income before other gains and losses).

Passive Income

In order to build reliable passive income streams, we must first understand exactly what the term passive income really means. Building online businesses that take advantage of systems of automation that allow transactions, cash flow, and growth to happen without requiring a real-time presence. In other words, we don't trade time for money. Instead, we internet entrepreneurs invest our time upfront creating valuable products and experiences. We work hard now to continually reap the benefits later.

What passive income is not

Let's dispel with some myths and set realistic expectations before we go any deeper.

1. Generating passive income is not easy and it takes a lot of hard work.

Nothing in life comes easy. Making money online is no different. Many conventional internet marketers and online entrepreneurs will try to persuade you to think otherwise. Why? Because they're trying to make money from false hopes. I'm here to tell you the truth: online business is hard. I'll do my best to guide you and give you the information you need, but I can't force you to take action; that's up to you.

2. Generating passive income does not happen overnight.

I don't live, teach, or believe in get-rich-easy schemes. My first online business took about a year of hard work before it was generating enough to support my family. There was nothing easy about what I had to do to get that business going. But in relative terms, it was "quick" because I decided to opt-out of the work till 65 deferred life plan and make my own luck happen. You can do it too.

3. Generating passive income is not impossible.

Passive income was just a dream for me until 2008. That's when I was let go from my job due to the crumbling economy. With no other options, I bet on myself by trying to make my dream a reality. And you know what? The dream came true, and it's totally awesome! I get to stay at home with my family, work when I want, and make my own decisions. This lifestyle is possible, and I want you to experience it too.

ANALYZING YOUR BUSINESS'S STRENGTHS, WEAKNESSES, OPPORTUNITIES, AND THREATS (SWOT)

SWOT analysis (Strengths, Weaknesses, Opportunities, and Threats) is a method of assessing a business, its resources, and its environment. Doing an analysis of this type is a good way to better understand a business and its markets, and can also show potential Investors that all options open to, or affecting a business at a given time have been thought about thoroughly. The essence of the SWOT analysis is to discover what you do well; how you could improve; whether you are making the most of the opportunities around you; and whether there are any changes in your market—such as technological developments, mergers of businesses, or unreliability of suppliers—that may require corresponding changes in your business. This actionlist will introduce you to the ideas behind the SWOT analysis, and give suggestions as to how you might carry out one of your own.

What is the SWOT process: The SWOT process focuses on the internal strengths and weaknesses of you, your staff, your products, and your business. At the same time, it looks at the external opportunities and threats that may have an impact on your business, such as market and consumer trends, changes in technology, legislation, and financial issues.

What is the best way to complete the analysis: The traditional approach to completing SWOT is to produce a blank grid of four columns— one each for strengths, weaknesses, opportunities, and weaknesses—and then list relevant factors beneath the appropriate heading. A rush of competitors into your area could easily represent a major threat to your business. However, competitors could boost customer numbers in your area, some of whom may well visit your business.

What is the point of completing a SWOT analysis: Completing a SWOT analysis will enable you to pinpoint your core activities and identify what you do well, and why. It will also point you towards where your greatest opportunities lie, and highlight areas where changes need to be made to make the most of your business.

What To Do

Know Your Strengths: Take some time to consider what you believe are the strengths of your business. These could be seen in terms of your staff, products, customer loyalty, processes, or location. Evaluate what your business does well; it could be your marketing expertise, your environmentally-friendly packaging, or your excellent customer service. It's important to try to evaluate your strengths in terms of how they compare to those of your competitors. For example, if you and your competitors provide the same prompt delivery time, then this cannot be listed as a strength. However, if your delivery staff is extremely polite and helpful, and your competitor's staff has very few customer-friendly attributes, then you should consider listing your delivery staff's attitude as a strength. It is very important to be totally honest and realistic. Try to include some personal strengths and characteristics of your staff as individuals, and the management team as individuals. Whatever you do, you must be totally honest and realistic: there's no point creating a useless work of fiction!

Recognize Your Weaknesses: Try to take an objective look at every aspect of your business. Ask yourself whether your products and services could be improved. Think about how reliable your customer service is, or whether your supplier always delivers exactly what you want, when you want it. Try to identify any area of expertise that is lacking in the business as you can then take steps to improve that aspect. For example, you might realize that you need some more sales staff, or financial help and guidance. Don't forget to think about your business's location and whether it really does suit your purpose. Is there enough parking, or enough opportunities to attract passing trade? Your main objective during this exercise is to be as honest as you can in listing weaknesses. Don't just make a list of mistakes that have been made, such as an occasion when a customer was not called back promptly. Try to see the broader picture instead and learn from what happened. It may be that your systems or processes could be improved so that customers are contacted at the right time, so work on boosting your systems and making that change happen rather than looking about for someone to blame.

It's a good idea to get an outside viewpoint on what your weaknesses are as your own perceptions may not always marry up to reality. You may strongly believe that your years of experience in a sector reflect your business's thorough grounding and knowledge of all of your customers' needs. Your customers, on the other hand, may perceive this wealth of experience as an old-fashioned approach that shows unwillingness to change and work with new ideas. Be prepared to hear things you may not like, but which, ultimately, may be extremely helpful.

Spot the Opportunities: Completing a SWOT analysis will enable you to pinpoint your core activities and identify what you do well, and why. It will also point you towards where your greatest opportunities lie, and highlight areas where changes need to be made to make the most of your business.

Watch Out for Threats: Analyzing the threats to your business requires some guesswork, and this is where your analysis can be overly subjective. Some threats are tangible, such as a new competitor moving into your area, but others may be only intuitive guesses that result in nothing. Having said that, it's much better to be vigilant because if potential threat does become a real one, you'll be able to react much quicker: you'll have considered your options already and hopefully also put some contingency planning into place. Think about the worst things that could realistically happen, such as losing your customers to your major competitor, or the development of a new product far superior to your own. Listing your threats in your SWOT analysis will provide ways for you to plan to deal with the threats, if they ever actually start to affect your business.

Use Your Analysis: After completing your SWOT analysis, it's vital that you learn from the information you have gathered. You should now plan to build on your strengths, using them to their full potential, and also plan to reduce your weaknesses, either by minimizing the risk they represent, or making changes to overcome them. Now that you understand where your opportunities lie, make the most of them and aim to capitalize on every opportunity in front of you. Try to turn threats into opportunities. Try to be proactive, and put plans into place to counter any threats as they arise. To help you in planning ahead, you could combine some of the areas you have highlighted in the boxes; for example, if you see an external opportunity of a new market growing, you will be able to check whether your internal strengths will be able to make the most of the opportunity. For example, do you have enough trained staff in place, and can your phone system cope with extra customer orders? If you have a weakness that undermines an opportunity, it provides a good insight as to how you might develop your internal strengths and weaknesses to maximize your opportunities and minimize your threats. The basic SWOT process is to fill in the four boxes, but the real benefit is to take an overview of everything in each box, in relation to all the other boxes. This comparative analysis will then provide an evaluation that links external and internal forces to help your business prosper.

What to Avoid

Focusing just on a few issues: Don't just focus on the large, obvious issues, such as a major competitor encroaching on your business. You need to consider all issues carefully, such as whether your Internet system provides everything you need or whether your staffing levels are as they should be.

Completing your SWOT analysis on your own: Do take advantage of other people's contribution when you're completing your SWOT analysis; don't try and do it alone. Other people's perspectives can be very useful, particularly as they may not be as close to the business as you are. This distance can often help them see answers to thorny questions more easily, or to be more innovative: we all get stuck in a rut at points.

Using your analysis for the next ten years: Don't do a SWOT analysis once and then never repeat the exercise. Your business environment will be constantly changing, so use SWOT as an ongoing business analysis practice.

Relying on SWOT to provide all the answers: Use SWOT as part of an overall strategy to analyze your business and its potential. It is a useful guide, not a major decision-making tool, so don't base major decisions on this analysis and nothing else.

GO FOR A DEMANDING NICHE

For many new businesses the question is whether they should target a mass or niche market. If you get the mass appeal right then you are guaranteed a high volume of sales. If you get it wrong you will disappear without a trace and are likely to lose money. Appeal to a niche and you create something that has a chance of standing out and this can be extremely cost effective as marketing spend is more targeted. Niche marketing refers to competing within a narrowly defined market segment with a specialized offering. The firm's competitive advantage comes from its expertise (as a specialist) and from having a high market share of a small market segment. As a result many potential competitors may not see it as viable to compete in niche markets. Achieving success as a niche marketer is a challenging and risky strategy. The major risk is that the business is reliant upon a relatively small market and is vulnerable to market downturns. However, get it right and there are many benefits including little or no competition, high profit margins, business stability from strong customer relationships and concentration of marketing spend.

Here are a few tips on how to create demand in a niche market:

Identify users' needs: By disrupting an established market, entrepreneurs can gain knowledge on what's missing in current offerings. Listen to consumers on social media and forums for complaints, demands and recommendations to discover untapped demand.

Make your product stand out: If you want to create demand for your product or service, you've got to offer something they haven't seen before. Whether it's a new experience, a twist on a popular product, an added service or aggregating information in a way that is useful for them. Focus on value creation by identifying your unique-selling proposition but also try to build a relationship with your customers.

Tell a story: If you are positioning your product to disrupt an established market, chances are you have a distinct offering. Tell people about it as consumers love a great story. By providing background information and a little narration, you can set yourself apart from every other company selling the same product.

Get the word out: Once you've developed a distinguished product or service, generate demand by creating a buzz. One low-cost strategy is to build up brand ambassadors; the people that can't stop talking about your product. Ask for their feedback, give them previews into new offerings and provide incentives to spread the word.

Online Niche Marketing: Some businesses exist only online to appeal to a specific segment or interest group; Mumsnet is a good example which provides parents with advice, the latest news, product reviews and discussion forums. These businesses make their money from advertisers who are keen to target their users. If you are thinking of developing a business in this area here are some issues to consider:

- Find niche keywords and check if there is sufficient demand

- Get a good domain name

- Spend time blogging

- Is niche marketing more profitable? It depends on how you do it. Like all marketing it takes time, money and skill to build a market and make a profit.

FOCUS ON YOUR STRENGTHS

Multiple studies have shown that people pay keen attention to negative information. For example, when asked to recall important emotional events, people remember four negative memories for every positive one. No wonder most executives give and receive performance reviews with all the enthusiasm of a child on the way to the dentist. Traditional, corrective feedback has its place, of course; every organization must filter out failing employees and ensure that everyone performs at an expected level of competence. Unfortunately, feedback that ferrets out flaws can lead otherwise talented managers to overinvest in shoring up or papering over their perceived weaknesses, or forcing themselves onto an ill-fitting template. Ironically, such a focus on problem areas prevents companies from reaping the best performance from its people. After all, it's a rare baseball player who is equally good at every position. Why should a natural third baseman labor to develop his skills as a right fielder?

The Positive Organization: Positive organizational scholarship (POS) is an area of organizational behavior research that focuses on the positive dynamics (such as strength, resilience, vitality, trust, and so on) that lead to positive effects (like improved productivity and performance) in individuals and organizations. The word "positive" refers to the discipline's affirmative bias, "organizational" focuses on the processes and conditions that occur in group contexts, and "scholarship" reflects the rigor, theory, scientific procedures, and precise definition in which the approach is grounded.

Used correctly, the RBS exercise can help you tap into unrecognized and unexplored areas of potential. Armed with a constructive, systematic process for gathering and analyzing data about your best self, you can burnish your performance at work.

Step 1

Identify Respondents and Ask for Feedback: The first task in the exercise is to collect feedback from a variety of people inside and outside work. By gathering input from a variety of sources—family members, past and present colleagues, friends, teachers, and so on— you can develop a much broader and richer understanding of yourself than you can from a standard performance evaluation.

Gathering Feedback: A critical step in the Reflected Best Self exercise involves soliciting feedback from family, friends, teachers, and colleagues. E-mail is an effective way of doing this, not only because it's comfortable and fast but also because it's easy to cut and paste responses into an analysis table such as the one in the main body of this article.

Step 2

Recognize Patterns: In this step, Robert searched for common themes among the feedback, adding to the examples with observations of his own, and then organizing all the input into a table. Like many who participate in the RBS exercise, Robert expected that, given the diversity of respondents, the comments he received would be inconsistent or even competing. Instead, he was struck by their uniformity. The comments from his wife and family members were similar to those from his army buddies and work colleagues. Everyone took note of Robert's courage under pressure, high ethical standards, perseverance, curiosity, adaptability, respect for diversity, and team-building skills. Robert suddenly realized that even his small, unconscious behaviors had made a huge impression on others. In many cases, he had forgotten about the specific examples cited until he read the feedback, because his behavior in those situations had felt like second nature to him.

Finding Common Themes: The RBS exercise confirmed Robert's sense of himself; but for those who are unaware of their strengths, the exercise can be truly illuminating. Edward, for example, was a recently minted MBA executive in an automotive firm. His colleagues and subordinates were older and more experienced than he, and he felt uncomfortable disagreeing with them. But he learned through the RBS exercise that his peers appreciated his candid alternative views and respected the diplomatic and respectful manner with which he made his assertions. As a result, Edward grew bolder in making the case for his ideas, knowing that his boss and colleagues listened to him, learned from him, and appreciated what he had to say.

Step 3

Compose Your Self-Portrait: The next step is to write a description of yourself that summarizes and distills the accumulated information. The description should weave themes from the feedback together with your self-observations into a composite of who you are at your best. The self-portrait is not designed to be a complete psychological and cognitive profile. Rather, it should be an insightful image that you can use as a reminder of your previous contributions and as a guide for future action.

Step 4

Redesign Your Job: Having pinpointed his strengths, Robert's next step was to redesign his personal job description to build on what he was good at. Given the fact that routine maintenance work left him cold, Robert's challenge was to create a better fit between his work and his best self. Like most RBS participants, Robert found that the strengths the exercise identified could be put into play in his current position.

Beyond Good Enough: We have noted that while people remember criticism, awareness of faults doesn't necessarily translate into better performance. Based on that understanding, the

RBS exercise helps you remember your strengths—and construct a plan to build on them. Knowing your strengths also offers you a better understanding of how to deal with your weaknesses—and helps you gain the confidence you need to address them.

CHAPTER 3:
HOW TO CREATE YOUR PRODUCT/SERVICES

Give customers what they love

Whether you refer to them as clients, customers or accounts, your experience working with any of these groups has likely presented you with the tough decision to either give a business what they want or to give them what they really need. If you are lucky, these two areas overlap and you look like a hero as you deliver favorable results to your smiling clients. All is right in the world! But sooner or later, after enough years in the business and after working with enough people, you will find yourself stuck between a rock and a hard place as you deal with clients who bring you ideas that you know are not going to help them achieve their goals. Henry Ford alludes to this conflict in his quote, "If I had asked my customers what they wanted, they would have said a faster horse." Often, customers are too close to their own business to see the bigger picture of what it really needs to get to the next level. They will ask for a bandage to fix a gaping wound, when really the underlying problem – and its solution – is much deeper.

So how do you gracefully persuade customers to accept your recommendations for what they need when this differs from what they want? Let's take a look at five steps that will get you headed in the right direction. Be kind, but honest when sharing your opinion and expertise. There is never a need to be rude or condescending when informing clients that you do not believe their ideas will achieve the results they desire. Remember, they have sought out your expertise because they want your input. Strive to build a relationship based upon kindness and honesty so that you are able to openly share your opinion and they are well received by your clients. The more your clients trust you and the more your track record of advice has panned out in their favor, the more likely they are to listen to your recommendations in the future.

Offer real examples backing up why something may not be in their best interest: Some clients will want to see proof as to why their idea is not good for their business. Do your research and offer real examples or statistics of other businesses that have used a similar idea or strategy only to have it yield less than desirable results. Another method is to back up your own ideas with research and examples. Don't just tell your clients; show them why you and many others have found your idea to be of greater benefit.

Get them excited about these options: Your clients may come to you with a "bad" idea because another business did it and it looked cool so now they want to do it too. They're excited about it and for that reason alone it's attractive. Use this "shiny object syndrome" to your benefit by turning your "better" options into other, shinier objects that catch their eye. Your excitement for these options will get them excited as well. Best of all, they should love that these ideas are new and different from what another business has already done. They will get to be among the first!

Offer praise and encouragement: Finally, step off your soapbox, get down from your high horse and take a back seat to receiving the glory when your ideas deliver the results you've promised to your clients. All the credit you could want will make its way to you in the form of a nice paycheck. Until then, be a cheerleader for your client and offer praise and encouragement for their smart decisions that have helped them to achieve their goal.

ASSESSING VALUE-IN-USE

The benefits customers enjoy are heightened by the experience of consuming and using your products and services. This is called Value-in-Use. Our study also showed that in a business-to-business context, the Value-in-Use varies from end-user to decision-maker. The research was undertaken in three phases. The first involved the application of an in-depth repertory grid case using a product-service supplier and its customer organizations. 39 repertory grids were generated, which elicited 411 Value-in-Use attributes. Second, a survey with 320 respondents (an even mix of end-users and decision-makers) was carried out to generalize the Value-in-Use findings from the previous phase. The final phase focused on the use of an analytical hierarchy process to help organizations make better decisions for improving the delivery of customer Value-in-Use.

The Outputs

The Workbook: Understanding the real value your customers get from your organization's product-service is the most powerful way to assess customer Value-in-Use, and focuses on analysis of the consumption process. The objective of this workbook is to provide you with clear, simple and reliable guidelines to help your organization assess your customers' Value-in-Use.

1. Key attributes that your customer appreciates from your product-service offering.

2. The most frequent attributes of your product-service offering.

3. The role of your attributes to develop a new contract and/or renew an existing one.

The methods described in the workbook require collaboration between customers and suppliers in order to achieve the best results.

The Management Tool: This Visual Demonstrator for Assessing Value-in-Use has been produced to help organizations to assess their customers' Value-in-Use. The objective of this demonstrator is to provide you with a simple tester to assess the Value-in-Use your customers are getting from your product-service offerings. This takes 8-10 minutes of your time. The tool uniquely assesses the customer's Value-in-Use through a psychology technique based on basic mathematical comparisons of different product-service suppliers

ENHANCING PRODUCT AND SERVICES

If you're looking to grow your business by improving your products and services, start by focusing on your existing customers and their needs. Talk to them, and find out their views on:

- what they're buying from you, and what they value most about it

- what you could do to make it more useful and valuable to them

- what would encourage them to buy more

Getting customer feedback should help you to identify ways to improve what you're offering to your current customers. It may also allow you to:

- increase the price you charge to your existing customers

- attract new customers whose needs you weren't meeting before

Try to ensure that any changes you make will increase your sales and profitability enough to make the time and money you'll need to invest worthwhile. If possible, you should test out prototypes of improved products or services with a few existing customers. By doing this, you can get their feedback and avoid making unpopular changes that could harm your business. Doing this is equally important for all businesses, whether you're starting up or established, improving an existing product or service, or bringing something new to market.

Think about selling online: Selling your products or services on the internet can:

- help improve efficiency and productivity

- reduce costs

- help you communicate better with customers and suppliers

You can use analytics software to help you understand how customers use your site and show you ways to improve it. The digitalskills.com guide can help you find out more about selling your product online.

Consider the costs of going online: You'll need to make sure you understand all the costs involved (e.g. hardware, software, hosting, training, services, maintenance and support, upgrades etc). You must also provide your customers with certain information.

Online security: If you're going to sell online, protect your customers and business with measures to keep systems and data safe from theft or hackers.

Develop new products and services: In business you can boost your product and services by initiating new products and services; this will help to expand your string of income and create new customers for patronage and increase your daily/monthly income.

Hire and train staff: As your business expands, you'll need more capacity to produce or provide your product or service, and a wider range of skills. The easiest ways of achieving this are usually by taking on new staff, or training your existing workforce.

Employing people: By taking on new people you can spread your workload, expand production and take advantage of new and different skills and expertise. This applies whether you already have employees, or you started your business on your own as a sole trader and are thinking about taking on staff for the first time. Find out about your responsibilities when employing someone.

Apprenticeships: Taking on an apprentice allows you to grow your capacity by investing in people who want to learn. Your business benefits from the skills they develop as they train both on and off the job.

Benefits of development

By developing new products and services, you can:

- sell more to existing customers (making the most of existing relationships is cheaper than finding new customers)

- spread fixed costs like premises or machinery across a range of products

- diversify the products you offer so you're less reliant on certain customers or markets

Another way of expanding your product range is by importing goods from overseas to sell in the UK. Make sure you know the rules on things like tax and commodity codes if you're planning to import.

WHAT IS PROTOTYPE AND HOW DOES IT WORK

One of the most frequent questions we hear from entrepreneurs is about the design cycle and how long it will take to develop an idea into a real product. Of course that answer totally depends on the complexity of the product, but by breaking the process down, there are solid ways of estimating what will happen and when. The cycle consists of three big loops -- design, engineering and production. The goal is to move gracefully from loop to loop, but you often need to run a loop more than once to get it right. Generally speaking, it's hard to develop a new product in less than six months. Nine to fifteen months is common, and many products take a lot longer. Let's make this concrete by using two hypothetical product examples: a cup holder that clips onto your bike and a pet food monitor that sends information about how much your pet is eating to your smartphone.

Design loop: Entrepreneurs most often come to us having already spent a lot of time thinking about their product and what they want it to do. This sometimes lets us bypass the beginning of the design loop, which involves product concept generation or user research to identify product opportunities. Instead, our first task is to build upon the vision to come up with a form, functionality and a way of making the product. We refine the idea through an iterative process of creative thinking, sketching and building 3D models on a computer. Photorealistic renderings and prototypes help zero-in on the look and feel. Ideally these product directions are tested in focus groups or using user research. If that isn't feasible, they are tested by the entrepreneur in more informal settings. If the product has a lot of inner mechanical or electrical components, we also spend time figuring those out. Does it need a screen? Buttons? A motor and gears? A way to weigh the pet food? A Bluetooth connection? Those parts get pulled into the design process so the final forms that are produced can practically fit both the user interface and the guts.

For a cup holder, this process could take two to four weeks. For a smart pet feeder, it could take four to six weeks.

Engineering loop: Engineers work with industrial designers throughout the design phase, helping behind the scenes and suggesting solutions for constraints. When the engineering phase starts, they hit the ground running, taking the design direction and turning it into parts that can be manufactured. If there are similar products we can get our hands on, we tear them apart to benchmark them. In our office, you better hold on to your stuff, or you may find it in our lab in a hundred pieces. Products with electronics, like the smart pet feeder, need additional work in terms of component selection, laying out circuit boards, and tackling the software. Electrical engineers work side-by-side with the mechanical engineers, integrating the two sides of the project as we go, making sure everything will work together. Software components tend to be the biggest wild cards: making them work well is time-consuming, and it is hard to resist adding features.

The engineering loop is about creating something that works, but also about making it the best it can be. We try to make the product light, sustainable, or cost-effective depending on the clients' priorities. If you don't anticipate high quantities, you might want to minimize tooling. If you anticipate making a lot, the cost of parts is more important to keep low. At the end of this loop, we build alpha prototypes that look and work like the product, but are not ready to be mass-produced. We test the alpha, go back and improve things, and then make a refined beta prototype, which is the last one before you move onto production. These prototypes are a chance to further debug the design, function and user acceptance of the product. For a cup holder, this process could take four to six weeks. For a smart pet feeder, it could take eight to 12 weeks.

Production loop: Sit tight. Entrepreneurs are often surprised by the length of this process. Finding vendors, documenting the design, waiting for tools, debugging the parts, and any required regulatory compliance always takes longer than you would like, but it is the final big loop and often what separates a good idea from a great product.

For a cup holder, this process could take six to 12 weeks. For a smart pet feeder, it could take four to six months. With each phase you are locking things in and investing more time and money. Your vision will evolve either subtly or radically as you go along. Like a rollercoaster, each loop prompts its own thrills (and terrors), but you won't end up in the same place you started. This is a good thing. Trust the process.

CHAPTER 4:
CHOOSING THE RIGHT CUSTOMER

All companies claim that their strategies are customer driven. But the term "customer" is among the most elastic in management theory. A working definition might be that your customers are the people or entities that buy your products and supply your revenue. That includes any number of actors in a company's value chain: consumers, wholesalers, retailers and so forth. Other definitions don't even require that a customer supply revenue. In fact, many business leaders believe that treating all value chain partners as customers improves internal coordination and responsiveness. The framework lays out four steps: identifying the best primary customer for your business, creating processes to learn what that customer values, allocating resources accordingly and building an interactive control process to monitor the assumptions that underlie your choice.

1. Identify Your Primary Customer

Identifying the best primary customer for your firm involves assessing each group of customers along three dimensions: perspective, capabilities and profit potential. Perspective refers to the culture, mission and folklore of a business, often revealed in stories about important events or people in the company's history. It is the lens through which executives consider opportunities and strategic direction. The choice of primary customer must reflect a company's perspective; otherwise the company will be unable to leverage the energy of its people in service to the customer.

2. Understand What Your Primary Customer Values

Once you've determined who your primary customer is, the next step is to identify which product and service attributes the customer values. Within the same industry, different primary customers may value different things: Some demand the lowest possible price; others want a dedicated service relationship. To complicate matters, customers often don't know exactly what it is they value. Uncovering the full truth about their needs requires systematic research.

Finally, you should set up processes for identifying products or services that customers may not know they need. Smart companies typically rely on ethnographic methods. At Procter & Gamble, for instance, where consumers are the primary customer, executives ask their managers and market researchers to spend days at a time accompanying consumers on shopping trips to more fully understand the extent to which various products meet consumer needs.

3. **Allocate Resources to Win**

Your choice of primary customer and your understanding of what the customer values provide all the information you need to make the critically important decision of how to organize your company's resources -in other words, what kind of business model to adopt. There are five basic configurations you can choose from.

Low price: If your primary customer is looking for the lowest possible price, centralized operating functions (such as merchandising and distribution) should receive the bulk of organizational resources, in order to create economies of scale and scope.

Local value creation: If your customer values products and services that are customized to local preferences and regulations, you should organize like Nestlé. It pushes resources out to regions so that local managers can customize product offerings.

Global standard of excellence: If your customers are looking for the best possible technology or brand no matter where they are located, you should organize resources around global business units that are defined by product lines.

Dedicated service relationship: If your customer is looking for a deeply embedded service relationship, you should organize like IBM. Customer teams in industry-based "verticals" marshal and coordinate product and service delivery from centralized, product-based "horizontal" units.

Expert knowledge: If your primary customer is looking for expert technical knowledge, you should follow the example of Google, where research and development sits prominently on top of product organizations that receive the lion's share of the company's resources.

4. Make the control process interactive

Your business model cannot survive forever. Customer tastes will change, new technologies will replace old and unforeseen competitors will enter the market. That means you must constantly gather information on shifts in your competitive environment, especially those that might affect the behavior of your primary customer. If the changes are dramatic, you may need to fundamentally reorient your business model -and even select a different primary customer. The best way to get the information you need is to make sure that your company's control systems are interactive. Depending on your business, you can choose to use any of your current management systems interactively -your profit planning system, brand revenue system or new deal system. The entrepreneurial landscape is littered with the carcasses of companies that tried to be everything to everyone. They muddled along until they were overtaken by crisis. It is ultimately less risky to be proactive and make the key strategic bet of choosing a primary customer. Companies that hedge their bets usually find themselves looking at the taillights of their more decisive competitors.

WHAT IS A POTENTIAL PROSPECT?

In the world of business marketing, the strategic focus has slowly shifted from seeking potential clients to making them want to come to you. In other words, you as a business owner can finally forgo the drudgery of always having to jump through hoops to gain a client and instead focus on making your customers want to come to you. To learn how to utilize this marketing strategy, read the helpful tips listed below:

1. Don't target everyone.

Admittedly, it does seem counterproductive to minimize your potential client base when attempting to grow your business. However, often catering to a niche client base will help you succeed in your efforts to grow your business, not the reverse. After all, you can't please everyone and people love specific personalized solutions for their problems. By selecting a niche group within your broad business arena, you can market more specifically and offer products or services for specific needs. A good example is Richard Simmons. He is known as exercise expert who focuses on a niche market: overweight people who would otherwise avoid working out. In so doing, Simmons has become a huge success.

2. Make your marketing entertaining.

While you want prospects to attain information about your business, product or service after watching the ad, you also want your marketing campaign to be memorable, funny and worth sharing. Otherwise, it will likely be forgotten.

3. Provide free resources.

If you as a business owner and solve a client's problem for free, you will have succeeded where 99.9 percent of others have failed. By offering a tip or helping a client pro bono, you are building repoire with them which could lead to business down the line. This can help gain credibility, trust and create an image of yourself as an expert in your field.

4. Use authority positioning.

Authority positioning means that you are seen as an expert in your chosen field. To communicate your trustworthiness to your clients, try the following strategies: Align yourself with other experts. Whether through speaking at the same seminar as other experts in your field or simply using their logo on your website (with their permission of course), when you align yourself with other experts in your field, you garner immediate trust. Share what you know through various means. Whenever you have an opinion, can offer advice or build yourself up as a thought leader share a lot and often. A great example of this point is Dave Ramsey. He shares what he knows about financial independence with Christian values on his radio show every day. He also uses seminars, books and his website, to build brand trust and recognition.

5. Create a strong digital profile.

Having a polished digital profile is an important step in getting prospects to come to you. Potential business connections and clients will sometimes search for your name in advance of meetings, so you want to have an impressive profile available for them to peruse. Your digital profile is a reflection of who you are, what you are passionate about and what you do well. In addition, since you should also include a photo in your profile, it shows your appearance. Your online profile allows you to brand yourself and showcase your talents, and in many ways, has taken the place of a traditional resume. A digital profile that is well maintained gives you the ability to create a professional network, which will help you build trust and authority in your field.

THE MARKET COMPETITION

Define your Brand

No two businesses are alike just as no two customers are alike, hence the need for branding. What does your business stand for? What's different about your business in comparison to other businesses in your industry? What do you want to be known for in the marketplace? Is there anything special about your business? You see when new competitions enter into your line of business, whether you like it or not, be prepared to loss some market share. I know that was rather harsh, trust me, it's for your own good. Don't take it personal, it's just the way the world is; different strokes for different folks. No one business can appeal to everybody. So your best response is to define your brand and consistently communicate your own Unique Selling Proposition (USP). The emergence of competitions clearly separates the men from the boys. It is the businesses that don't clearly stand for something that often get eaten up by competitions. If your business doesn't stand for something, it will fall for anything.

Our brand became so unique that 'Yahoo Yahoo boys' (internet scammers) literally avoided our cybercafé. From the outset we didn't do overnight browsing. Somehow without us saying a thing or imposing any law, just by our commitment to our brand, they realized our cybercafé wasn't the right place for them to carry out their nefarious activities.

Choose a Competitive Advantage

Jack Welch, the former CEO of General Electric (GE) was right when he said "if you don't have a competitive advantage, don't compete". In other words, don't bother getting into the game if you haven't first figured out a plan on how to win. There are basically 3 key areas to focus on when choosing a competitive advantage;

- Quality: You can choose to beat the competition by offering a superior quality than others.

- Price: you can choose to beat the competition by offering the lowest prices

- Service: or you can choose to beat the competition by offering an unforgettable customer service.

Most of the time it is not so easy to measure up well on all three key areas. However, it's important to include service in any of the combinations you want to focus on. Why? The other two forms of competitive advantage can cost you a lot and often time customers can choose otherwise. There's always an alternative to quality; if you focus on only offering the highest quality at a premium price, customers will scout around for a lower quality at a cheaper price. There's always an alternative to price; if you focus on offering the cheapest price possible it will require that you find a way to drive down your cost to the barest minimum. And this can turn out in form of low quality products or services and customers will start to complain.

What do you do

Pick either of the two; price or quality as your competitive advantage and complement it with service. Without the element of service in your competitive strategy you can never deliver happiness to your customers. People may not remember how great your product or service is (quality); they may not remember how much you made them pay (price), but they will never forget how you made them feel (service). You see it is possible for your competitions to copy your products or services just in our case they copied our pricing plan, timer, banner etc. but they couldn't copy the way we treated our customers and the spirit and attitude of our workers. Our greatest strength was hospitality, they just couldn't beat the way we made our customers feel whenever they visited our cybercafé. And when we surveyed our customers, asking them what made them stick to us, they kept saying the way we treated them was exceptional.

Create a Customer Database

Do you know that it cost 20 times more to get a new customer than it cost to keep an old customer? Customers are very expensive to attract and that is why smart businesses focus on a customer's lifetime profitability (CLP) rather than on a one-off purchase. This means that they place more emphasis on building an enduring relationship with their customers rather than on making a sale. They have realized that it is wiser to have their customers for life; rather than having them for a while. Why? Because your greatest success in business will come from the number of repeat purchases you're able to generate from your loyal customers. This is how the concept of relationship marketing came to be –building a long term profitable relationship with your customers.

This was the idea behind our membership strategy: We were more concerned about keeping our customers for life (building a relationship) than keeping them for a while (making the sale). As a result we were able to convert 80% of first time visitors into registered browsers in our cybercafé. Initially it seemed like a lot of work and a lot of cost on our side, but on the long run, the benefits outweighed the cost and the efforts expended to create our own customer database through the membership strategy. Our greatest strategic weapon against our competitions is our customer database (membership strategy).

There is nothing more powerful than having a communication link between you and your customers. It is the cheapest but most effective tactic against intense competitions.

The following two points will explain better how we creatively used this tool against our competitions.

Communicate 'WITH' and 'TO' your Customers

If you are not talking with and to your customers, someone else is. This is a very vital element in your response to competitions. Talking 'to' your customers is what is known as advertising and talking 'with' your customers is what is known as market research. A lot of small businesses undermine this very important marketing strategy of constantly communicating to and with their customers. Haven't you realized this is the key behind the marketing success of most big companies? You should see how much big companies spend on advertising and market research, maybe then you would better appreciate the value of communication. This was a major component of our response to the competitions. We didn't relent in sending out messages via SMS (mobile marketing) to our customers every first day of the month and on every major public holiday. We kept in touch with them constantly updating them with vital information and words of encouragement to help them hang on through the economic recession.

Why? Because of our membership strategy (customer database).

We didn't just talk 'to' our customers; we also talked 'with' them through periodic customer satisfaction surveys that we conducted. Talking to your customers is a good thing, but talking with your customers is a great thing. Why? Talking with them helps you better understand them which in turn help you serve them better. To show our customers how much we wanted to talk with them through our customer satisfaction questionnaires, we paid them in kind with a 3 hours ticket every time they filled the questionnaire. Through these surveys we were able to know those specific things they liked about us and wanted us to continue no matter what. Also, we were able to know those specific areas they wanted us to improve on in order to serve them better. And lastly, we were able to know those specific things they wanted us to stop doing that they didn't consider added value.

Excite your Customers

People will no longer have cause to deal with a business that isn't innovating. Innovation brings excitement to the marketplace and customers like excitement. Take time to study the reaction of people whenever a company is about to launch a new product, service or brand, you would be thrilled at what you would discover. Innovation gives the marketplace something exciting to talk about. And there is nothing that drives a business faster than word of mouth advertising. If you can find a way to get your customers excited enough to talk about your company as a result of the innovative things you consistently come up with, then you've got an edge over the competition. You become the pacesetter of your industry. Others will literally look up to you and can only follow your lead. We were able to achieve this with our customers through our monthly promotions. In a bid to increase sales we decided to come up with at least one new promo for our customers every month. We literally gave them something to talk about every month. We came up with promos such as: "tell a friend promo", "Buy one get one free promo", "Heavy browsers promo", "Early bird promo", "weekend promo", "Facebook promo", "Scanning promo", "Fill a form promo" "Laptop promo" and so on.

KNOW YOUR COMPETITOR CUSTOMERS

Whether you want to admit it or not, competitors are out there and they're hungry for your customers. While it might seem unfair given everything else you need to keep on top of in building up your business, you might want to consider devoting the time and energy into keeping tabs on your competition. "By monitoring competitors on an on-going basis you get to know their behavior and so can start to anticipate what they will be likely to do next," says Arthur Weiss, managing director of UK-based Aware, which helps businesses gain competitive intelligence. "You can then plan your own strategies so that you keep your customers and win (not steal) customers away from competitors." In other words, keeping tabs on your competition is a great strategy for growing your business.

The good news is that while hiring someone like Weiss can save you or your employees from spending the time to conduct research on your competitors, you can also employ several techniques to get the job done virtually for free. Here are 10 tips from entrepreneurs and small business owners on how you can start gathering information on your competitors.

1. **Go beyond a Google search.** There's no doubt that any research project these days should begin with a simple Google search or visiting your competitor's web page. But there are also a variety of tools either supplied by Google or that relate to Google's search results and Ad Words campaigns that might give you interesting insights into your competition. For example, Sheel Mohnot of FeeFighters, a comparison shopping website for credit card processing, says he uses the following tools to keep an eye on his competition:

Do some reporting: There are great and inexpensive resources for checking up on your competitors online and offline. "I recommend routinely tracking what the industry analyst firms like Gartner are reporting about your industry, as well as trade associations and advocacy groups," says Becky Sheetz-Runkle, author of Sun Tzu for Women: The Art of War for Winning in Business. "These organizations are doing research and studies that evaluate the people who are and should be your competitors. What are they telling you about where the industry is trending? Where are the unmet market needs that you can fill?"

Tap the social network: Of course, given how companies are increasingly using social networking sites like Facebook, LinkedIn, and Twitter as marketing outlets these days, you might be able to pick up interesting facts about your competition—and maybe even your own company—just by tuning in. "We find that monitoring tweets, Facebook posts, blogs, and other new media mentions of our competition is an easy, cost-effective way to stay in tune with and in the know about the public's sentiment about our competitors," says Michael Meschures, the president of Spaphile.com, a weekly deals site that shares high-end spa and beauty offers. "In a similar vein, we track our competition by keeping a very close eye on review sites, such as Yelp and Citysearch. We scour through reviews to find mentions of our competitors' deals, and then target that particular Yelper or Citysearcher's other favorite businesses so we're always one step ahead of the competition." Even if your competition isn't social media savvy, it's a good bet that they produce newsletters—either e-mail or print varieties—that you can sign up for to get the latest and greatest news and updates on things like new products or services they are introducing and what events they might be attending.

Ask your customers: When it comes to identifying sources of information about your competition, don't skip over the obvious ones—like your customers. "Speaking to customers is one of the best (and cheapest) ways of gathering real information on competitors," says Weiss. "Whenever you win a new customer, find out who they used before, and why they switched to you (i.e. The reason they were dissatisfied with their previous supplier). Do the same when you lose a customer—identify what they preferred about your competitor. If you gather enough of these stories you'll get a very clear idea on what competitors are offering that customers view as preferable. You can then adjust your own offering to beat that of the competitor."

Attend a conference: Attending industry trade shows and conferences—as well as joining industry associations—can be a great way to learn about who your competitors are and what they're offering, says Amy Lewandowski, who heads up marketing at online retailer, PepWear. "We attend these conventions anyway so we make sure to visit competitors' booths while we are there and observe their interactions with customers, pick up literature, and check out the quality of their products," she says. "I am always shocked that most of them never visit our booth."

Check in with your suppliers: If you work in an industry where you share the same suppliers as your competitors, it could pay to ask them some simple questions. "Talk to your suppliers and spend time getting to know them," says Zach Berning, co-owner of Overland Gourmet. "While they may not tell you what your competition ordered or their volume, ask better questions." For example, if you ask them how many units of a certain product have been pre-ordered for the next month, you might find out not only what your competition might have ordered, but what other products your supplier might be bringing in as a result.

Hire your competition: Another strategy is to hire employees from competing firms—especially sales people—and team up with competitors' partners, suggests Sheetz-Runkle. "No one knows more about the inside of those organizations than the employees," she says. "Find out all that you can about how these companies operate, and more importantly, what's on the horizon for them? Where are they taking their business? What markets are they venturing into? How are they leveraging innovation to cut costs and advance productivity? Where is the highest level of dissatisfaction with their products or services? No one has more and better intelligence when it comes to sales than disgruntled sales people."

Watch who your competitors are hiring: You can also learn something by studying the kinds of jobs your competitors are looking to fill, says David B. Wright, the chief marketing officer at W3 Group in Atlanta. "For example, if a company is hiring a programmer, they will include information about exactly what technologies the candidates need to know, which tells you what they use," he says. "Also look at what positions they are hiring—if they're looking for a patent attorney, they could be working on some big new inventions. If they're hiring for several HR, they may be preparing to expand overall."

Conduct a survey. If you're interested in getting a comprehensive report of all the players in your industry, you might consider conducting a survey. "A year or so ago, I hired someone to e-mail several of our competitors and ask them the same questions about their services," says Jeff Huckaby, CEO of RackAid, an IT management business in Jacksonville, Florida. "We looked at price, response time, how the sales request was handled, etc. By doing this, we learned how to clearly differentiate our sales process from that of our competition." While Huckaby says he learned a lot from the process and plans on doing it again, he does have one caveat: "I am a big fan of outsourcing this. You don't want to run into someone you were spying on at an industry conference."

COMPETITIVE PRICING

Do you know how much your products are worth? How low are you willing to price an item to compete with another ecommerce retailer? With the advent of highly competitive pricing tools, winning the online pricing war can be a lose-lose for ecommerce retailers. Large online retailers like Amazon have an advantage in competitive pricing, as they can set the price low enough to run smaller retailers out of business. But there are other ways to compete - and it all starts with developing (or at least thinking about) an ecommerce pricing strategy. Here are

6 tips that will help you develop an ecommerce pricing strategy:

Know your Margins: The reality of online retail pricing is that the lowest price doesn't always win. In fact, pricing battles usually end with you pricing your products too low. Even with enough customers, you still may not make a profit. If you are lowering your prices to a point where you are losing money, you should consider finding a better source, or adjust your product offerings to include more profitable items.

Know your USP (Unique Selling Proposition): What makes us different? Every company has to tackle this question to determine their value proposition and target market. For online retailers, a unique factor could be excellent customer service (i.e. Zappos), free or timely S&H (i.e. Amazon Prime), or product you can't find anywhere else (DODOcase). Of course, there are many more.

Loss-Leader (Selling Below Market Value): Highly discounted pricing can be advantageous if paired with the appropriate merchandising strategy. The Lose-Leader Strategy assumes that an item sold below market value will encourage customers to buy more overall. Using this strategy, online store owners have the opportunity to upsell, cross sell and increase the total shopping cart value (average revenue per user).

Offer Incentives: Once you know your margins, and price accordingly, then you can offer incentives to motivate your customers to buy. Even if you can't sustain an ultra-low price in the long term, you can always offer limited time pricing to reach these customers. For example, "Purchase in the next hour and receive 20% off!" Being savvy with your incentives allows you the ability to garner attention to your products, and build a reputation for having good deals, without breaking the bank.

Diversify Product Offerings: To offer a diverse product offering that will sell, ecommerce store owners must first understand their market demand. Make sure that you are up to date with current trends by reading ecommerce news. Use products like "Google Trends" or "Google Insight" to check the popularity of a SKU and try to attend local Meetups with fellow online retailers.

Test your Ecommerce Pricing Strategy: As with many things in ecommerce, one size does not fit all, so it is important to measure and test the success of changes you make to your online store's pricing strategy. Ideally, every change should be tested and validated with an analytics tool (i.e. Mixpanel, Google Analytics, and Shopify Sales Dashboard). For example, find out if your 'Summer Sale' (where you implemented one of these strategies) increased your conversion as you expected, or if the new, trendy products in the store are generating more profit than older products.

CHAPTER 5:
SELLING YOUR PRODUCTS/SERVICES

Many copywriting and marketing gurus teach simplistic ideas about psychology. They insist that people can be fully understood and manipulated with a checklist of motivators or pyramid of needs. What nonsense! I can't even figure out why the guy at the pet store puts 75 cat food cans in one bag and a tiny box of treats in another so that I lurch to my car leaning to one side. How can I possibly summarize human psychology in a few bullet points? People are highly complex and often mysterious, so we all struggle to understand our fellow humans. However, now that you've gotten over being afraid to sell, here are a few basic psychological tidbits that can help you write compelling copy.

People make decisions emotionally: They decide based on a feeling, need, or emotion, not through a logical thought process. That's why intangible benefits are the keys to persuasion. When you're writing, you should ask yourself, "What is the emotional hot button here?"

People justify decisions with facts: Example: a man sees an advertisement with a photo of a sports car and instantly falls in love. However, he can't bring himself to buy the car based on a feeling, so he reads the copy for technical details about the powerful engine, safety features, and low maintenance. He wants the car because it makes him feel good. But he buys it only when he can justify the purchase rationally.

People are egocentric: The word "egocentric" means centered on the ego or self. We all see the world in terms of how it relates to us personally. So when your copy asks someone to do something, it must also answer the unspoken question, "What's in it for me?" On a deeper level, the question might be "How does this give me feelings of personal worth?"

People look for value: Value is not a fixed number. Value is relative to what you're selling, what others charge, what the prospect is used to paying, how badly the prospect wants it, and how the prospect perceives the difference between your offer and others. You must demonstrate a value that seems to be equal to or greater than the asking price. The greater the value relative to the price, the more likely people are to buy.

People think in terms of people: The human brain is not a computer, calculator, or information processor. Scientists have shown that its primary function is to deal with social interactions. Remember how some mathematical questions in high school were stated as real-life situations? They were always easier to understand and solve than abstract problems. Your copy, therefore, should feature people through names, personal pronouns, quotes, testimonials, stories, photos of satisfied customers, etc.

You can't force people to do anything: When people buy, it's not because you wield some magical power over them. You can urge. You can push. You can entice. But ultimately, people do what they want to do. This means your job is to show how what you're offering meets your prospect's needs.

People love to buy: Some say people don't like to be "sold." Not true. People love to be sold. They love to discover wonderful new products and experiences. What people don't love is to be cheated or tricked. Therefore, it can be helpful to change your analogy of the marketing process. Instead of "selling" to people, try to "help" them. Sell good products, make appealing offers, and treat people fairly. That's a surefire formula for success.

People are naturally suspicious: It's true that there's a sucker born every minute, but most people are moderately skeptical of any offer. They seek to avoid risk. You can never predict the level of suspicion any particular person has, so it's usually best to back up all claims with evidence, such as testimonials, survey results, authoritative endorsements, test results, and scientific data.

People are always looking for something: Love. Wealth. Glory. Comfort. Safety. People are naturally dissatisfied and spend their lives searching for intangibles. At its simplest, writing good copy is a matter of showing people how a particular product, service, or cause fulfills one or more of their needs.

People buy "direct" because of convenience and exclusivity: If people could easily find the things you offer at a nearby store, that's probably where many would buy them. So if they are not buying from you directly for sheer convenience, they're doing it because they can't find the item elsewhere (or just don't know where to look). That's why it's wise to emphasize the convenience and exclusivity of what you wish to sell.

People like to see it, hear it, touch it, taste it, or smell it before they buy it: Some people never buy online because they can't examine the merchandise. Some items, such as books and CDs, are tangible and familiar enough to sell easily online because there is little doubt about the physical quality. Other items, such as clothing or food, may be a harder sell — at least until people have a satisfactory buying experience — because quality may be variable. Think about how people buy things in stores and ask yourself if there is some element of that sensory experience that is missing from your sales message.

Most people follow the crowd: We look to others for guidance, especially when we are uncertain about something. We ask, "What do others think about this? What do others feel? What do others do?" Then we act accordingly. This is why testimonials and case histories are so influential. Of course, this barely scratches the surface. Psychology is a deep and eternally revealing line of study. And while I don't believe in making things more complicated than they have to be, I think there is great benefit in knowing not only what people do, but also why they do it.

IDENTIFYING THE OBSTACLE

As a salesperson, you will put in a lot of time and effort to ensure that your product or services are needed by your prospect. Yet, no matter how compelling the need, no matter how precise the definitions of what is desired and required, prospects will naturally have objections, concerns, and requests for additional information. Nevertheless, you should welcome objections because once answered, they give you the potential energy to close the sale.

Before Getting Started: In selling, one definition of an objection, is "a reason given by the prospective customer why they are not ready to buy your product or service." Sales courses teach you that an objection is an obstacle to be overcome. They also teach that every objection can be answered. Many people use objections to avoid making decisions or commitments and not necessarily because they don't want to buy what you are selling. However, when your prospect doesn't have any objections, you might be facing your most difficult close. Your success as a salesperson will depend on your ability to anticipate and handle a prospect's objections. No matter how good or thorough you may think your presentation is, at some point, your prospect may throw an objection at you, and how you handle it will make the difference on whether you close the sale or not.

Anticipating Objections: New salespeople dread objections because they are not sure they can find convincing arguments to counter them. However, seasoned sales veterans have learned how to take the prospect's objection and turn it around in order to close the sale. As a sales professional, you will probably put a lot of time and effort into developing a winning presentation to ensure that your product or service is needed by the prospect. Yet no matter how precise your presentation and no matter how compelling you have presented the prospect's need for your product or services, there might be objections, concerns or necessity for additional information.

An easy exercise for you to do before you make your presentation is to review it in detail. When you get to a point where you think there might be a customer objection, write it down on a separate sheet of paper. Continue doing this until you have reviewed the entire presentation. Once you have finished, give your presentation to a friend, asking him to give you any objections that come to his mind. You might find other areas of objections to work on before delivering your presentation to a prospect. When you think you have exhausted all of the possibilities where objections could originate, continue to work on the solutions. Practice your answers. You may not be able to come up with all of the answers to make your presentation "objection proof," but you will surely have a handle on the presentation and be loaded with answers in the event the questions do come up.

The ability to anticipate an objection is very important but not nearly as important as developing the skills necessary to overcome your prospect's concerns. No matter how hard you try to list every possible objection a client may have, there will still be those times when the prospect will have an objection that you never considered.

The inner workings of an objection: The term objection has an additional meaning to the one given earlier. As used here, an objection refers to "any hindrance voiced by the prospect which prevents you from moving to the next step in your presentation or closing the sale." The key word here is "voiced." Later on we will discuss "unvoiced objections." Usually a lack of understanding on the part of the prospect is the reason for the objection. Luckily, objections have a structure which can enable you to analyze them, determine the cause, minimize their occurrence and deal with the effects that arise. It is important to work with the prospect to understand the exact character and extent of his objections. Using a client-centered approach where you provide all of the facts necessary will work well in overcoming the objections. When you welcome objections you are communicating to the prospect that his needs are important and will be addressed. Examples of this approach would be: "I understand what you are saying. Another client asked the same questions. Here's how I worked with him to satisfy his concern..."

Honesty will take you far in your sales presentation. Don't tell the prospect what you think they want to hear. Today's prospects are far better prepared and more practical than in the past. If you listen to the prospect and acknowledge his objections as being valid, you will be offering additional justification for the prospect to buy into your product or service.

There are five steps in dealing with objections:

1. Expect them and allow the prospect to express them freely.

2. Welcome them when they occur because they indicate an interest on the part of the prospect.

3. Affirm the objection by restating it in the form of a question to be answered. "So what you are saying is that the delivery schedule is a concern to you, isn't it?"

4. Give complete answers to the objections. Draw upon testimonials, past experiences or whatever relevant information you have.

5. When the prospect presents an observation that's perceived as a real drawback, present an offsetting benefit such as, "Your concern about our plant location is justified, but we have air freight service to this area every day. Your orders will be delivered on time."

Do not respond immediately to a prospect's objection. Very often he will continue talking to clarify his position or to offer more information. When this happens, wait a few seconds and think about what he has said. Your pause shows a level of respect for what the prospect said.

Objections which face salespeople the most are:

1. Skepticism

2. Misunderstanding

3. Stalling

The best way to handle objections is to appear as a knowledgeable, interested salesperson whose mission is to help the prospect achieve his objectives and goals. Respond to objectives positively and respect the prospect's actions as legitimate concerns.

1. Skepticism

If the prospect seems skeptical about your presentation or your ability to deliver, it could come from one of the following situations:

- Promising too much. If you promise too much too soon or trivialize the uniqueness of the prospect's situation you will surely lose him.

- Failing to gain a rapport. You must listen and respond effectively. If the prospect thinks you are patronizing him or saying what you think he wants to hear, his interest in you will diminish rapidly. Learn to listen and respond effectively.

- Not asking the right questions. Know enough about the prospect's needs to be able to ask probing questions. Asking good questions is just as important as giving good answers.

- Not fully answering questions. The prospect's questions are real. Try not to think that any of them are "dumb questions," and do not avoid a question because you think it is trivial. By not answering all questions, the prospect could think you are trying to hide something.

- Coming off as defensive. If you appear to be defensive to an objection, you might turn him off completely. Given a choice, you should choose to be responsive. Always respond enthusiastically, not defensively.

- Not client-centered. If you speak in general terms and do not address the specifics of the prospect's objection, you have not given him the answer he is looking for.

- A perceived lack of time. If you rush through your presentation or do not give enough consideration to the prospect's concerns, you could make the prospect feel uneasy. Don't linger endlessly on any one point, but don't give any quick answers either.

2. Misunderstanding:

These objections fall into three categories:

Inadequate definition of the need: A good salesman has the ability to define and solve problems. By understanding the prospect's situation, you are better able to offer the help or answers he needs. Take the time to get the facts and offer the solutions necessary to close the sale.

Inadequate goal definition: You have to know what the prospect's goal is before you can try to suggest a path. If his main concern is to produce 2000 units in a month and your product is a critical part in the units, speak in terms of providing the parts to do that. Don't try to improve his procedures. Help him to hit his goal.

Inadequate definition of benefits and features: You must provide specific examples of how the prospect will benefit from your product or service and your proposed solution to his objections. Do not give global answers to specific problems

3. Stalling

If the prospect seems to be stalling, the reason might be one of these:

He is not the decision maker: If this is the situation, find out who the decision maker is and ask to meet with that individual. This can be done by asking the prospect himself or trying to gain the information from the receptionist. A simple question, such as, "Mrs. Smith, I sell color copiers. Can you tell me who the person is that is in charge of specifying and buying color copiers?"

He's not sold on your product: Ask probing questions to determine what the problem is. "Are you not sure about our pricing?" "Is it your concern about our ability to deliver?" "What is holding you back in making your decision?"

He wants to get other proposals: Find out what his criteria are in the proposals. Also, see if you can determine what kind of information he is looking for. Ask if the project is going to be awarded on a competitive bid basis only. Try to be the last bidder to present.

He's too busy to talk right now: Ask him what his schedule is and when you can return or call him back. Also, it might be good to find out if the project is a reality and not just a fire drill.

The project is not budgeted: An excellent chance for you to show him cost benefits and be willing to adjust your scope of work to fit his time frame. "You have told me that his project has not been budgeted for this quarter. However, I can see that you need our products. I have spoken to our financial people and we are willing to invoice you at the start of the next quarter if you agree to receive a shipment within ten days."

WHAT ARE THE RISKS OF BUYING FROM YOU?

Any time customers consider purchasing a new product or signing up for a new service, they also face a set of uncertainties about the product or service collectively referred to as perceived risk. As part of the conversion process from potential customer to paying customer, businesses must develop strategies to assuage one or more of the six types of perceived risk.

Functional Risk: One of the most common types of perceived risk, functional or quality risk refers to the fear that a product or service will fail to deliver promised functions or benefits. A new computer, for example, might fail to run the resource-intensive, audio editing program a sound engineer needs to perform her job.

Social Risk: Social risk refers to the possibility that buying a product or using a service can reduce a person's status with friends, family or neighbors. If, for example, someone purchases a pure-bred dog and finds his friends consider adopting animals from shelters the socially responsible behavior, he suffers a loss of status.

Financial Risk: Financial risk boils down to a fear that a potential purchase can tax or outstrip a person's monetary resources, now or in the future. Financial risk operates on both a subjective and objective level. A person with low or variable income can experience a high level of subjective financial risk, even with low-cost items. The purchase of a home, on the other hand, often means an objectively high level of risk, even for those with stable finances.

Physical Risk: Physical risk refers to the perceived potential for a purchase to cause bodily harm to a person or loved one. A firearm, for example, might create a high level of perceived physical risk in the minds of some customers. A book or magazine, by contrast, prompts physical risk concerns in few customers.

Time Risks: The increasing pace of contemporary life means more customers worry about time risks, in particular time lost when a product turns out to need replacement or fails to deliver as promised. It can also include pragmatic concerns about how much time you might spend waiting in line at a crowded retail outlet. Many businesses seek to alleviate this concern by offering online purchase options on their websites or through online retailers.

Psychological Risks: Consumers also face questions about whether a given purchase is the morally right choice. For example, a customer may want to buy from a particular company because it offers inexpensive alternatives, but feel ambivalent due to the company's labor practices.

HAVE A CUSTOMER REFERRAL PROGRAM

People would rather do business with people they know--or know of--than with strangers. When you're introduced to a prospect through a personal recommendation, that prospect has a vastly higher comfort level than, say, a buyer you find through cold calling. After all, few things are more reassuring than a positive endorsement from someone you know and trust. So why is it that, while we all covet referrals, we don't pursue them as much as we should? I think it's largely a matter of developing good habits.

Change Your Thinking: Imagine your business as an infinite web of relationships. Every one of your business contacts has the potential to connect you to dozens of other contacts. The relationships are out there, but they'll likely remain out of reach unless you actively pursue them. It may never occur to your current contacts to broker an introduction. It's up to you to put the idea in their heads.

Don't feel sheepish about asking for referrals: there's nothing pushy or smarmy about it. People won't give you referrals unless you deserve them. In fact, getting a referral is the highest compliment you can receive. Let your customers know you prize referrals, which you'll earn by providing excellent quality products and services.

Make It a Habit: I know one entrepreneur who built a successful business almost solely on referrals. How'd he get so good at it? When he was an eager young sales apprentice, his manager trained him well. Every time he glanced at his watch, which he did often in his zeal to stay on schedule, it meant it was time to ask for a referral. Eventually, it became second nature.

HAVE A CUSTOMER REFERRAL PROGRAM

When you begin working with a new customer, make referrals part of your initial agreement. "If I do a great job for you--and I will--you agree to give me X number of referrals." Chances are your customer will be impressed by your dedication and drive.

Whenever a customer compliments you, respond with a thank you, quickly followed by a referral request. For example, "I'm so pleased you're happy with my work. Do you know anyone else who can benefit from my services?"

Use every client meeting as an opportunity to collect referrals: To keep yourself on track, jot a reminder down in your meeting preparation notes. Make it one of your standard talking points.

Set a weekly goal for yourself: Keep track of the number of referrals you ask for each day. You don't need to limit your requests to clients; you can also ask business associates, acquaintances and prospects.

Make the most of every networking opportunity: Step out of your comfort zone at networking events and set a goal to talk to at least three new people. Plan in advance what you might say. We're all drawn to interesting, enthusiastic people.

Always be specific when asking for a referral: Looking for high net worth individuals? Say so. Interested in midsize companies? Let them know. If you don't tell your contacts who your target customer is, you'll waste time pursuing leads you can't use.

Give and You Shall Receive: One of the most powerful ways to elicit referrals is to give them generously yourself. Whenever you have the opportunity to refer an associate or bring two contacts together, do so. And when you're attending the aforementioned networking event, make a point of introducing people to one another. Most people will appreciate the referral, and it may inspire them to respond in kind.

One last thought: Always thank someone who has given you a referral. Send them a note, keep them informed of your progress and maybe even treat them to lunch. What's the close ratio on referral business, compared to other prospecting methods? I don't have a definitive answer for you, but I've seen estimates that range from 50 to 500 percent more. Those are big numbers. Whatever that number is for you, you can bet it's a whole lot higher than cold calling, advertising, web marketing or virtually any other sales technique you might employ.

HAVE A CUSTOMER LOYALTY PROGRAM

Customers are the bread and butter of any small business, and winning people's long-term loyalty can really pay off for you and your business. It is well documented that the majority of a firm's sales come from a small proportion of repeat customers. Experts also estimate it costs between two and 10 times more to win a new customer than to retain an existing one. Targeting these loyal customers can help boost your sales and gather more names in your customer management software for future marketing efforts.

Why set up a loyalty program: According to Jupiter Research, approximately 75 percent of consumers have at least one loyalty card. When implemented well, these programs can benefit both customers and businesses alike.

Shows customers they are valued: It is one thing for a business to say "thank you" at the bottom of every invoice or receipt and another thing to communicate that feeling by giving a customer special offers and perks. Make people feel special for doing business with you.

Encourages return business: When people have a number of options to choose from, sometimes the mere knowledge they may earn a reward from a particular retailer is enough to influence their choice. If you place particular limits on your program - such as an expiration date - you may also be able to encourage people to shop sooner rather than later.

Helps you gather information: You can collect information from the members of your loyalty program to learn more about your customer base. For example, some programs offer you the opportunity to track customer spending habits with your customer management software and gather data on demographics. Members of your loyalty program may also be more likely to return a customer survey and provide useful feedback.

Low-cost advertising: If customers see your name on a membership card whenever they open their wallet or on an email when they check their inbox, you are taking advantage of low-cost advertising. Additionally, the information gathered from these programs can help you plan out your marketing budget by identifying who is more likely to spend.

Setting up a loyalty program: Let people opt in. If you want high participation in your program, let people opt in. On your website or at your cash register, give customers the option of filling out a form to join your loyalty program, with the promise of receiving regular or occasional special offers form your business. Keep track of these email addresses with your customer management software.

Keep it elite: If you want to limit participation to those customers who spend the most, you could consider offering invitations to a select few.

Issue membership cards or numbers: Create a real or virtual membership card that customers can use to track their purchases and work their way up to a discount. Membership cards can be a major influence on customers' behavior. After all, if they know it will take just three more purchases at your business to earn their reward, why would they go anywhere else?

Send regular emails: Set up an email newsletter to communicate with loyalty program members so they feel like they're part of an elite group. These emails can be filled with useful content, descriptions of new products and special offers.

For example, if you sell body care products, your email newsletter might contain tips on how to deal with dry winter skin, an explanation of the ingredients in your newest body wash and a coupon for 5 percent off of the customer's next order.

How to structure rewards

Buy nine, get one free. This is the method used by a number of coffee shops, which give visitors their 10th drink free. You can use this as a model and tailor the specifics to your business.

Discounts: Particularly if you run a service-based business, it may make sense to offer a discount on future orders to customers who spend above a certain amount. For example, award a 10 percent-off coupon for every $100 customers spend in a single order.

Clubs: Most supermarkets offer a club-style rewards program, which tracks their purchases and permits certain advertised deals only to those who are a member. This method may work well for businesses that are keen on targeted advertising.

Rewards for paying upfront: Small business owners can offer their regular customers an incentive to pay ahead. This can also help with cash flow management.

Contests: You could hold regular contests to write reviews for products, come up with ideas for the regular email newsletter - or simply hold a raffle for all customers who spend more than a set amount in a given month.

CHAPTER 6:
MARKETING: FINDING YOUR TARGET MARKET

How to establish your target market

If you've just launched a startup, you've likely spent a lot of time planning and building your business. Part of that planning process involves—or should involve—deciding who will be on the receiving end of your marketing efforts. Your products might appeal to a large group of people, but it doesn't make sense to try to market to everyone. You obviously want as many people as possible to know about your business. But the more potential customers you want to reach, the more time and money it's going to cost to do so. Defining a target audience might feel constraining to you, but just remember that you're not excluding anyone; you're choosing where to spend your time and money. Selecting a target audience will help save you resources. Focusing on a portion of the people who might be interested in your products will allow you to communicate and engage with that segment more deeply. Below is how your plan gets stated:

Consult your business plan: Look at the goals you've set for yourself and analyze the products and/or services you offer. Think about how your products or services fulfill a need or solve a problem for a potential customer. Also, think about how you differ from other companies in your industry—what makes you stand out? Broadly think about who might be interested and who may benefit from having access to what you offer. Figuring out your selling point is the first step in identifying your ideal target audience. Next, think about what information you need to know and why. What do you need to know about your potential customers in order to reach them? As you consult your business plan and decide who you want your audience to be, remember that it is ultimately about the customer. Don't think about who you would like to sell to, think about who is looking for the products and services you offer.

Begin researching: Start with secondary research. There are a lot of existing sources that can help you pull together information about your industry, the market, your competition, and the broad potential customer you have already identified. The best part is that someone has already done the work and, in many cases, the information won't cost you anything. The downside is that the information may not be focused in a manner that is 100% useful for your purposes. Nevertheless, it's always a good idea to do some searching. You never know—the research you need may indeed exist. If you're unable to identify secondary data that is useful for you and you have the budget to do so, you may want to conduct primary research. This could involve surveys, interviews or even focus groups. Though primary research can be expensive, it could allow you to get answers to questions specific to your business.

Develop a customer profile: After performing research, you'll want to create a customer profile. This is more than a brief statement; it's an in-depth description of who your typical customer may be and includes demographic and psychographic information:

Demographic information: This may include age, gender, location, ethnic background, marital status, income, and more.

Psychographic information: This type of information goes beyond the "external" and identifies more about a customer's psychology, interests, hobbies, values, attitudes behaviors, lifestyle, and more. Both types of information are essential for developing your customer profile. Demographic information will help you identify the type of person who will potentially buy your products and services. Psychographic information goes one step further and nails down why that potential customer may buy

Find out where your audience is: It's not enough to just say who your target audience is. Find out which websites they visit and which social networks they most frequently check. Are they glued to their email? Are they addicted to apps? The information you put together for your customer profile, combined with knowing where your audience hangs out online or how they use technology, will facilitate the delivery of your message.

Monitor and evolve: The work doesn't end after you've identified your target audience. It's essential to continually perform research to stay current on market and industry trends and your competition. It's also important to see if and how your current and potential customers evolve. Before you begin marketing to your potential customers, make sure you know how you are going to track sales, interactions, requests for information, and more. All of these touch points are important to record. This information will help you identify trends, patterns, and possible areas of improvement, which will continually help your marketing efforts as your business matures.

BUILD A LEADING LIST CONTAINING YOUR TARGET AUDIENCE

While the first article was concerned with identifying your target audience, this second part looks at ways to start communicating with your audience to make them aware of your practice and how you can be of benefit to them. You've decided what type of clients you want to attract to help grow the practice, so how do you go about 'targeting' them? If you've explored all the options for getting introductions to these prospective clients, i.e., introductions from your staff, current clients, business contacts etc, you're going to have to identify new methods of communicating with them.

Get to know their interests: Rather than jumping straight in with a mailing or a cold call, first try to find out where these clients 'hang out', i.e., where do they carry out their business. For example, do they attend networking groups, local business functions, awards ceremonies, charities or sports events and so on? If so, could you get involved with these events, whether by attending or becoming a sponsor, or organize a similar event which you could invite your targets to? Whatever you do it's about raising your profile in the 'space' your target occupies, in order to bring them closer to you. While we're not suggesting you stalk your potential clients, do remember that people buy from people. Identifying any shared interests will make it easier to start a conversation and develop relationships with potential new clients.

Pinpoint their issues: When you start communicating with your target audience it's important to put yourself in their shoes. Try to understand what opportunities or problems they may have, such as: getting to grips with the new auto enrolment plans; or trying to grow their business but needing external funding to do so. Marketing is about being in the right place at the right time. So if your conversation at an event touches on one of their issues, or a mailing or email you send them identifies that you can help them, it is more likely to produce a positive response. One further thing to bear in mind when communicating with your target audience is timing and frequency. You would be very lucky to have only one conversation or send just one mailing which results in sign ups. In practice, they will want to get to know you better first, develop a rapport and start to trust your expertise, professionalism and judgment.

Create a plan: It's important to develop a 12 month plan for targeting prospective clients, so there is a drip feed approach to them receiving information from your practice which demonstrates your credibility, problem solving abilities and the personality/culture of your practice. The best way to 'map out' your communications is to create a 12 month marketing calendar which contains details of which target audiences you intend to communicate with each month and what methods of communication will be used. The 12 month calendar can help you spread your marketing activities (and their costs) across the year, while assisting you with maximizing their effectiveness and keeping a steady trickle of communications going out to your targets. The same exercise can also be used for planning ongoing communications with your existing clients.

In conclusion: The key to communicating with your target audience is to focus your marketing activities on places where they go, i.e., you need to find a way so they notice you. On top of this, you need to understand what their issues are and how you can help them and to make sure all your marketing activities demonstrate this

HOW TO IMPRESS YOUR AUDIENCE

It is not the employer who pays the wages. Employers only handle the money. It is the customer who pays the wages. Those were the famous words from Henry Ford. Jeffery Gitomer's said on customer loyalty and its relationship with customer satisfaction and whoa, he's got some super principles that I really connected with. He also added don't be fooled by the signature at the bottom of your payroll check – the guy who signed the check didn't put the money there – your customers did.

One that really stood out for me was this principle – Your Customer is your Paycheck. With no customers, there is no money to pay you. He goes onto say that without customers, you're not getting paid, your business is worthless, and your wallet is empty. I think this is a great point and really flips the angle on customer service. If we treated all customers like they were our boss, we would go out our way to make sure their experience with us was 10 out of 10.

WAYS YOU CAN IMPRESS YOUR CUSTOMERS:

1. Thank all your customers for their business, and mean it

This is pretty straight forward. Be thankful for your customers continued support and business. Without their purchases and repeat purchases, you wouldn't be receiving your paycheck.

Saying thank you goes a long way to showing you appreciate your customers. And... an appreciated customer is a happy customer.

2. Go out of your way to help your customers

Jeffery mentions in his book that customer service should be renamed to customer help. If every time you interacted with a customer and you thought help rather than service, I can guarantee your customers would have had a better experience.

Try going out your way to help your customers. You will be surprised how thankful they will be for your extra help, not to mention the customer loyalty it will build.

3. Try to impress your customers, like you want a raise

Remember every time you tried to impress your boss by going out your way for something, or making sure you met some deadlines that seemed out of reach? Well... try doing that for your customers. Act like your customers are your boss, and do everything you can to impress them as if you wanted a raise.

4. Think about your paycheck every time you talk to a customer

Next time you check your bank balance after pay-day or receive your hard copy check, think about whose money that really is. Think about your customers.

5. Keep your promises and integrity

If you told your boss you would have some work done by close of business Friday, you'd make sure it's done wouldn't you. Well, the same goes for your customers. If you promise to call them at 4.30 – make sure you call them then, not 5 minutes later or the next day. Integrity goes a long way to building customer loyalty.

In wrapping this up, I'm probably going to have a few people yell out and say, as if my employees care that much about our customers!

Well, I'm here to tell you that is what you should be aiming for. Businesses need to look at ways to create a customer-focused cultural, where employees to treat customers like the kings. Because let's face it, at the end of the day... your customer is your paycheck.

CHAPTER 7:
MANAGING PEOPLE

Employees

All companies want to improve employee productivity, but how often do they examine their own management practices as a means of attaining it? Studies consistently show that a disturbingly high number of non-management employees are disengaged, not working at full productive capacity. Following are 7 practical suggestions – steps management can take to improve productivity by putting employees in a more productive mindset. Design economic incentives so employees at all levels of an organization can benefit from them. There's a natural tendency for management to focus most heavily on senior-level economic incentives. While this is completely understandable, it's best not to neglect substantive incentives for lower-level employees... that is, if you expect them to be vigorously committed to an enterprise's success. To the argument that this will be unduly costly, a program has to be carefully structured, of course, so additional payouts reflect clearly defined revenue and/or earnings targets.

Provide meaningful feedback in a constructive manner on a regular basis. Feedback is a foundational management skill; the ability to provide regular, helpful feedback to employees in a manner that encourages, not discourages, and is a cornerstone of effective management. That's not to say feedback is always positive – that wouldn't be management at all – but that the communication is done thoughtfully... whether the occasion is encouragement for a job well done, or that course correction is needed. Respect employees as individuals, in addition to the job they do. Respect can be a simple but powerful motivator, just as its unpleasant twin, lack of respect, has the opposite effect. When employees feel genuinely respected (always assuming it's warranted), they're much more likely "to go the extra mile" to help a company succeed.

Be sure management at all levels of an organization receives adequate training. There's a tendency for companies to invest heavily in "leadership training" while focusing far less on supervisors and middle managers. I can readily speak from experience on this one, having received considerably more training and development opportunities in the latter stages of my career than in the early formative stages, when I most needed it.

Why Employee Development Is Important, Neglected and Can Cost You Talent

Provide support for employees when it's genuinely needed. Valued support can take many forms: equipment when existing is outdated or inefficient; emotional support in the face of (occasionally) unfair criticism; flexible support for a reasonable level of work-life balance. Management support in times of need won't be forgotten; it builds employee goodwill and loyalty. Don't be emotionally stingy. There's nothing for management to gain by withholding praise and recognition when it's warranted. A recent employee study I came across indicated that recognition is often a more powerful motivator than money. While this may well be less true at senior levels as financial rewards escalate, this post is focused on general employee productivity...where the broadest gains can be made

Clients

So much work goes into winning new business, regardless of the vertical space in which you work; there is the initial prospecting, early conversations, strategic program development, budget consideration, and creation of a deliverables timeline. Unfortunately, all of that work can come to a screeching halt before the ink is dry on the contract when the same amount of time, energy and commitment isn't placed on managing the client's expectations after the business is won. To ensure this is never overlooked, we developed the Super Six: keys to developing excellent client expectations and building longstanding relationships that can withstand good times as well as bumps in the road. After all, it's easy to keep a client when things are going well; maintaining a client when times are tough is the true test of a relationship. We believe the Super Six will aid in this process:

Build a relationship that goes beyond client/vendor: I have long maintained that business people like working with people they not only respect, but also personally like. Therefore, we believe that developing a personal relationship goes a long way in building a stronger business relationship. Get to know the client's family situation, how they spend their free time, where their interests lie and, most importantly, what motivates them on a daily basis. When you understand what makes them tick as a person, you can translate that into your business relationship.

Regularly communicate and address problems directly: A lack of communication is usually at the root of most problems associated with clients. Any good client relationship will be able to weather setbacks if you are proactive in communicating both good and bad news. When communication is direct and transparent, trust forms and helps to create a foundation for long-lasting relationships.

Agree on strategy, goals and timelines: Until you and your client agree on strategy, goals and timelines, you are always at risk of them not understanding what success is and how it should be measured. We always suggest creating a scope-of-work document that outlines the program details, budgets and metrics. This will alleviate any confusion over expectations and hopefully eliminate a difficult conversation.

Be a counselor: When you offer your client advice, direction, input and business counsel, you become a truly valuable partner. This style of open dialogue helps to establish the respect necessary to ensure better project management. Clients hire outsourced marketing services because they want an objective opinion. If you fail at giving that POV, you subject yourself to being a "yes man or woman," which will ultimately be your undoing.

Be a good listener: Listening is one of the most misunderstood and least used tools in managing client expectations. Many clients are unsure of what they are trying to accomplish or not very good at articulating it. As such, you must have excellent intuition and listening skills in order to identify key messages being communicated. One of the best ways to compensate for a client who communicates poorly is to repeat what you have heard and ask them to confirm the accuracy of key takeaways, which will ultimately impact expectations.

Budget is not a bad word: Most relationships will go south very quickly if you are not open and honest about budgets. To start, you must be realistic about setting a clear understanding of the budget required to execute the desired program. Throughout the course of the program, you must have regular dialogue about budgets. If you don't address the client until you have an issue (i.e., operating over budget), you will not only have an unhappy client, you may also find yourself eating the overages. At the end of the day, your ability to manage client expectations is going to hinge on how well you choose to communicate. If you leave things up to chance, chances are you and your client will both be disappointed. However, if you take the time to listen, be proactive about communicating openly and address any issues head-on, you will keep client expectations in check and be in a good position to grow your relationship over time.

MANAGING THE UNEXPECTED

One of the greatest challenges any business organization faces is dealing with the unexpected. For example, a leading manufacturer of integrated circuits expects to boost competitiveness by dramatically improving quality and doubling capacity, but it unexpectedly finds its share price falling as customers switch to the new products being offered by its competitors. A premier forest products firm continues production during a normal trough in the business cycle, only to be surprised by a deeper and more long-lasting trough than they ever expected. The responsible manager of the largest corporate division of a consumer products firm suddenly realizes that his market has been conquered by a certain competitor—a development that his subordinates suspected had been building steadily for several years. As these examples show, the unexpected doesn't take the form of a major crisis. Instead, it is triggered by a deceptively simple sequence in organizational life: A person or unit has an intention, takes action, misunderstands the world; actual events fail to coincide with the intended sequence; and there is an unexpected outcome.1 People dislike unexpected outcomes and surprises. Because of that, they sometimes make situations worse. That's the tragedy that motivates this book.

We suspect that the inability to manage the unexpected lies behind a number of the pressing problems that executives face. Problems, after all, occur either when something that we expected to happen fails to happen or something that we did not expect to happen does happen. For example, consider the chief concerns of today's business professionals reported in the first annual (2000) University of Michigan Business School Pressing Problems survey. The second most frequent problem executives reported was "thinking and planning strategically"; the third most pressing problem was "maintaining a high-performance climate." From our perspective, both these problems are variants of one that is the focus of this book, dealing with unexpected events. Whether the issue is strategy or performance, problems become more pressing when expected strategy and performance outcomes fail to materialize or when unexpected impediments to strategy and performance materialize. Either scenario is a brush with the unexpected. And in either case people often take too long to recognize that their expectations are being violated and that a problem is growing more severe. Moreover, once they belatedly recognize that the unexpected is unfolding; their efforts at containment are misplaced

FINANCIAL GROWTH

One area many business owners struggle with is keeping track of their finances, but it is one of the most important areas given that cash flow is the lifeblood of the business. Small mistakes and a lack of knowledge and resources can be costly and problematic. We've selected some of the most important things to consider and provide these tips and resources. Find the best local credit union. Given their frequent willingness to provide loans, finding a credit union that understands the needs of your business can go a long way. There are many online tools to find credit unions based on specified criteria. Many local credit unions require membership in an affiliated organization, often listed on their web site, but costs to join are usually minimal and well worth it. Here are a few tools to start with: Find a Credit Union, Credit Unions Online or Credit Union National Association.

Find a trusted mentor. Access to free help is just a click away, with sites that help connect entrepreneurs with mentors fitting their needs. Having a mentor assist with setting up finances can be invaluable if the person is trustworthy. One resource is the Association of Small Business Development Centers, which provides access to full-time business counselors around the country, often former entrepreneurs or M.B.A. graduates. Other sites for finding mentors include SCORE (affiliated with the Small Business Administration), iMantri and MicroMentor. Choose the correct accounting software. While software is a mainstay of small business finance, sorting through dozens of choices isn't easy, since there may be better options for your specific needs than the popular QuickBooks program and related packages. Find Accounting Software is a free tool that helps find exactly the right solution through a detailed questionnaire. TaxSites provides extensive resources including a list of software for small businesses.

Consider hiring a bookkeeper. A good, trusted bookkeeper can handle all of the mundane tasks that go along with keeping finances on track. Be sure to understand the various types of bookkeepers and how to avoid fraud. A free bookkeeper hiring test (to be taken by prospective hires) can be requested. Accelerate cash flow with mobile payment systems. Mobile payment systems can allow faster and easier acceptance of payments for products and services. A system called GoPayment from Intuit allows acceptance of payments through mobile phones and can directly download the data into QuickBooks. To monitor transactions, users can access Intuit's online Merchant Service Center to search, view and create reports.

Look into factoring receivables. Accounts receivable financing allows immediate payment for invoices rather than waiting 30 days or longer and tying up working capital as a result. Factoring services advance the amount of the invoice minus a "discount", or fee (advances of 80 to 90 percent are common), and provide a "rebate" when invoices are paid – the amount depends on how long it takes the customer to pay. Factor Find provides a directory of factors specializing in small businesses. Businesses can be matched with the most appropriate factors at the International Factoring Association, BuyerZone, and Resource Nation. Understand and measure capital versus operational costs. The goal often is to drive down the totals on the capital costs side of the spreadsheet and move more over to the operational side of the equation. Operating costs don't require complex depreciation calculations and are more easily adjusted from year to year. Outsourcing is one way to do this because it sits on the operating cost side and helps to free up cash by not tying it up in capital investments (such as IT infrastructure, servers, etc.) or tasks like head hunting and payroll management. Measure bottom line impact by looking at the service budget year over year. Are the costs for delivering a service going up, staying the same or dropping? Figure out how much it costs to deliver specific services to the business such as recruitment, payroll or benefits management. Understanding cost-to-serve offers the business great insight into projects and tasks, how long it actually takes to do them, and as a result how much they cost. If you want to pare back on the budget, there are hard numbers to work with that show exactly what the impact on quantity and quality of service will be if resources are reduced.

FINANCIAL CONTROL

The moment you lose control of business cash flow, you're entering a danger zone. That is why it is essential for even the smallest commercial operation to have basic financial controls. These help you to retain a grip on your cash by reducing the risk of it being lost through inappropriate or ill-judged actions. Here are our recommendations for simple financial controls which every firm should consider implementing.

Cash flow planning: While keeping track of your cash is essential, it's also important to predict where it's coming from and where it will go. That's what cash flow planning, or forecasting, is all about. A cash flow plan is your estimate of cash flow movements over the weeks and months ahead. It should extend several months into the future, in order to give you an indication of when your cash could be at dangerously low levels. You should update your cash flow plan at least every month, to take into account changing circumstances.

Approval of purchases: Exercising firm control over spending can make a huge difference to your cash flow. Consider requiring all purchases to go through an approval process. This ensures accountability and encourages people to think twice before committing to expenditure. Putting delays into the buying process can give you time to consider less costly alternatives. You may discover that while something appears to be an urgent need, in a few days time, you realize it wasn't required after all.

Approval of payments: Your business will need to pay suppliers, HMRC and various other organizations. While the timing of many controls will be dictated by legal or commercial deadlines, it's still good practice to have a payment approval process. This reduces the chance of payments being made in error, or too early. If you have several people in your business, consider requiring two signatures on cheques or to approve online payments.

Control petty cash: The humble petty cash tin might never contain large amounts of money, but that doesn't prevent it being a drain on your cash flow. If possible, avoid having one altogether. But if it's needed to fund purchases of small incidentals, ensure that all cash payments are matched with receipts and that these are checked and accounted for on a regular basis.

Regular reporting of debtors and creditors: It's easier to remain in control of your cash flow when you know how much you are owed, and how much you in turn owe to others. If you use a computerized accounting system, this information should be easy to get hold of and should be reviewed on a regular basis. Having regular reminders of your debtors will help you to stay on top of credit control, reducing the risk of debts going bad by having been left for too long.

A clear expenses policy: Expense payments are another way for money to slip away, almost unnoticed, and uncontrolled, from your business. If you have staff, make it very clear who is entitled to make expense claims and for what and the process for doing so. Have strict limits on how much can be claimed for different types of activities, and ensure that all claims are approved by yourself or another senior manager. Unfortunately, some employees do abuse the expenses process, giving in to the temptation of round up mileage claims or add unreceipted costs.

CUSTOMERS' DIVERSIFICATION

With the recession appearing to recede, many companies are looking to expand their roster of paying customers, reaching in to new segments, covering a larger geographic footprint, and going after business that only a few months ago seemed all but unattainable. If you have a plan of attack using proven strategies, growth and expansion for your business are within reach. Show me a company with more than 10 percent of its business with one customer or more than half of its business in one industry and I'll show you a company at risk of being impacted by one company or one industry, says Paul Weber, CEO of Entrepreneur Advertising Group in Kansas City, Missouri. "Show me a company with a comprehensive social media campaign but ignores other media and I'll show you a company missing part of their audience. Show me a company only devoted to networking and I'll show you a company that will soon find their time availability slipping away." Weber's point is that frequency and diversity are essential in keeping any company viable and relevant with customers and potential customers. These are common problems for small businesses, but they are easily addressed. Here are five strategies to help you expand your audience and drive transactions with new customers.

Diversifying Your Customer Base: Try Cold Calling: When I've tapped out social networking, non-client referral sources, client referrals, sponsored or hosted events, webinars, article placements and blogs, I'll make cold calls, says John Thomas, a former director of business development in Dallas. "Sometimes they are to prospects and sometimes to potential referral sources. I've won a lot of business through a cold call."

Martha Retallick, a website developer and photographer for Western Sky Communications in Tucson, Arizona agrees, "I do most of my business prospecting via the phone. There's a lot of rejection out there. But you know what? Getting past the fear of rejection was surprisingly easy." The best way to get over your fear of cold calling is to practice. Look through your address book and start with clients you haven't done business with in awhile and expand to people beyond your immediate network.

Diversifying Your Customer Base: Ramp Up Your PR: Getting attention from the media is like getting free advertising on TV, in the newspaper, or via social media channels, allowing you to reach not only your current audience, but also people who may have never heard of you or your product, says Wendy Duval, public relations and communications manager for The Vermont Teddy Bear Company. "Much of the attention we've gotten from the media has been the result of releasing relevant products when the time was right. For example, designing Star Trek Bears around the time of the new movie's release or designing bears to represent all of the candidates during the 2008 presidential election." By making products relevant to current news topics, Vermont Teddy Bear was able to target their media outreach accordingly, which in turn resulted in increased visibility to a larger network of consumers.

Diversifying Your Customer Base: Turn Your Virtual Audience into a Real Audience

So, everyone is talking about social media. Why? Because it works. Social media is a cost-effective way to build up a new virtual audience. But your new audience doesn't have to stay virtual. Ted's Butcherblock, a full-service butcher shop in Charleston, South Carolina, knows a thing or two about turning social media followers into real customers. "We love to make fun offers with social media," says Ted Dombrowski, owner or Ted's Butcherblock. "We did one offer through Twitter that said, 'Be the first to come in and say 'I love bacon!' and you will win free tickets to our special bacon dinner.' I was shocked to see how many people came in the shop shouting 'I love bacon!'" For Dombrowski, social media was a great way to pull in a different demographic. "Social media was a way for us to reach out to a younger audience. We could use social media to make our shop accessible to a completely new type of customer."

Diversifying Your Customer Base: Focus on Networking: According to Caroline Nuttall, publisher of CHARLIE Magazine, "In a time when social media is king, real life, face-to-face networking goes a long way." Personal connections are a great way to increase your audience. It is easy for someone to forget an email, but it is much harder for someone to forget you, especially if you make an impression. "Speaking engagements are a great way to network, which allows you more of a mass appeal," says Nuttall. She recently spoke at a cultural event and said it was "a powerful speaking opportunity in front of a big crowd, the exact right audience for you, in a unique and memorable format. Sharon Kraun, former sustainability practice leader at Cohn, Overstreet & Parish Integrated Marketing in Atlanta has had to rely on the good old-fashioned way of person-to-person networking particularly for her start-up Marketing Matters. "Most of my business comes through referrals. Each successful client is a link to another potentially successful client, says Kraun. "While social media does enable you to reach more people in a shorter span of time, the one-on-one, in person communication still provides a stronger connection." Take every opportunity you have to talk about your business. People can't support what they don't know about.

Diversifying Your Customer Base: Embrace Your Competition: You don't have to fight your competitors for their audience; working together can often be much more efficient. The National Building Museum in Washington, D.C., uses this philosophy to broaden its reach both locally and nationally. "Through partnerships with like-minded organizations such as The American Institute of Architects and sponsors such as The Home Depot Foundation, the museum has increased national recognition of the organization by opening access to our partners network of supporters and members," says Johanna Weber, the museum's marketing and communications manager. "This in turn has resulted in increased web traffic, attendance at museum programs and exhibitions, and new fundraising opportunities for the museum." Partnerships go both ways, so if you are willing to help out your neighbor, you have to opportunity to gain the support of a much larger network.

CHAPTER 8:
FINDING AND RETAINING GOOD EMPLOYEES

Identify a good employee

Among the handful, or perhaps hundreds, of employees at your company, it can sometimes be tough to identify who are the high-potential employees that are really making a difference in your overall success, and who are the employees that are simply at or below average. You want to know who your high-potential employees are so you can reward them and make sure they stay in your organization. What exactly do top employees offer, and how can you identify the characteristics of a good employee?

What High-Potential Employees Offer a Workplace: Do you fret over losing your top employees? Feel confident you're paying and managing them better than anyone else in your industry. View our webinar Employee Retention: High Impact Performance Management for Engaging and Retaining Your Top Performers and get ahead of the competition. High-potential employees are catalysts in the workplace. They have a collection of qualities that influence the employees around them in positive ways. Here are some key characteristic of a good employee that you should look for.

Key Characteristics - What Makes a Good Employee?

- Work harder yet smarter than the average employee

- Inspire other employees by not being afraid to ask questions or to throw out new ideas

- Look for ways to innovate

- Contagiously motivate others with their energy, curiosity and by being an example for others

- Are self-starters and are critical to a healthy and productive workforce

- Just How Valuable Are High-Potential Employees?

Did you know that, according to an article in Human Resources Magazine, "End 'Equal Treatment' Today! Focus on Top Performers," top employees typically produce up to 12 times what the average employee produces? Now that's bang for your buck and let's face it - who can't use a heavy hitter like that on their team. Considering the current economic environment with hiring freezes, pay cuts, and employees doing more work with fewer resources; we need to retain high-potential employees now more than ever. While there are lots of articles out there that tell you how to attract top performers to your business, I want to discuss how to find them within your business now. You need to learn the best ways to identify top performing employees in order to retain them.

How to Notice Certain Types of Top Performing Employees: There are a number of different methods for identifying high-potential employees and top performers in your current workforce. Often, top performers will bring themselves to your attention by standing out from the crowd. Through their actions and the way they interact with peers, handle themselves in meetings or talk about their workload, you will find them. Here are some common traits of these obvious leaders.

Characteristics of a Good Employee: Push themselves and you for more work, bigger challenges and opportunities for development. Aren't afraid to speak up and give their ideas for improvement

Reliable and hard working: Employees, managers and customers tend to enjoy working with these individuals because they can count on them to get the work done and done right

How to Identify Less-Obvious High-Potential Employees: While the more outgoing, outspoken and gregarious top performers can be easy to recognize, some of their counterparts are not as apparent. These high-potential employees are hidden gems just waiting for you to notice them. They are very similar to other top performers except that they are subtler about their accomplishments.

How to Identify Quieter Top Performers

Discovered through metrics: Metrics they influence could be dashboard reports that show the quantity of product produced, quality of service, customer service surveys, etc. They have solid reputations and receive great feedback from other employees, managers and customers

A Classic Approach: Can I Live Without This Employee?

If you're still having trouble identifying high-potential employees and top performers within your company, there's another simple technique you can use. The quick and cheap way to identify top performers is by a simple force-rank of your employees. Ask yourself who in your department you can't live without and you will see your best employees bubble to the top of your list. It's also a great idea to have other managers and employees do the same. You can collect their results and compare. This is very telling. Force ranking is an informal way to find your top performers and one that I like since I subscribe to the KISS (keep it simple stupid) approach to most things. If you like a more formal approach then I would recommend the 360 review where you get similar information but with more structure.

Remember Your Goal: To Build a Stronger Company: No matter what size your organization is and how much you expect to grow in the coming years, having good employees in your company who are highly productive, self-motivated, meet deadlines and charge up your workforce with their enthusiasm is essential to your success. And, now that you can recognize the characteristics of a good employee in your department or company, you can take steps to retain these high-potential employees. That's another post...

WHAT DO EMPLOYEES WANT?

We've broken down the things employees want that will help you keep them on board.

Employees want purpose: Don't assume that a hefty paycheck and regular bonuses are the most important things to your employees. They, like you, want to know that what they're doing on a daily basis has some purpose behind it. "What people want most is the chance to make a difference," says Alexander Hiam, the Massachusetts-based author of Business Innovation for Dummies. "When you have a chance to have your ideas heard and one of them actually gets implemented, it's such a boost."

Building a culture of employee appreciation: Employees want goals. To instill a sense of purpose in your employees, be sure to lay out a clearly-defined set of goals for them on a regular basis. At Meddius, Gunther's team of managers re-aligns each department's goals every three months. "The goals have to be very measurable, obtainable goals," Gunther says. For the sales team, for example, that might mean setting a goal as to the number of deals the team is expected to close in a certain period of time for a certain dollar amount. Once goals are in place, it is up to each team to decide how to achieve them.

Employees want responsibilities. Sometimes the hardest part of being a manager is delegating, but employees crave your trust, and with that trust, should come responsibility. "People are so busy and harried themselves that all they do is work, they don't really manage," Hiam says. "Ask people if there are more things they can do, and then you can catch your breath and be a manager."

Employees want autonomy. Take it from Gunther, giving your employees freedom over how they work can actually make them more productive. Unless you're managing an assembly line, give your employees the freedom to work in a way that works for them. Daniel Pink, the Washington D.C.-based author of Drive: The Surprising Truth about What Motivates Us says, "Let people figure out the best paths to the goal, rather than breathe down their necks all the time."

Employees want flexibility. In addition to deciding how they work, the experts say employees also appreciate having a say over when they work. Gunther has, of course, set up a radically flexible schedule for his employees that might not work for every office. But, he says, it has enabled him to find and retain top talent for Meddius. "We've had people who have taken significant pay cuts to work for us, because at their old job they were told to show up and be at the office between 8 a.m. and 5 p.m.," he says. "Generation Y is looking for a synergy between their personal lives and their professional lives." Set up a flexible vacation policy or a telecommuting policy that enables employees to work from home. It involves a great deal of trust, but, as Pink says, "If you don't trust your employees, you've got much bigger problems."

Employees want attention: Just because you're giving employees the control they crave doesn't mean they don't want guidance and feedback. Hiam suggests checking in with them every few weeks, even if it's just for a minute or two. "Look them in the eye and ask how things are going. Find out what's really going on in their world," he suggests. "Responsibility is about giving them a chance to make a difference, but attention is the human dimension of managing." And don't be fooled into thinking that the traditional annual performance review is your big chance to tell your employees what's working and what's not. In Pink's words, "There's no way to get better at something you only hear about once a year." That's why, at Meddius, Gunther uses the year-end to make decisions about promoting employees, and uses the quarterly meetings where goals are set, to address big operational issues within each department.

Employees want opportunities for innovation: Not long ago, Google announced its 20 percent creative time policy, which encourages employees to work on any innovative ideas they have that are company-related during 20 percent of their hours at work. Both Hiam and Pink applaud this concept. "People need to be given a chance to bring about something new and exciting," Hiam says. "Just asking people for ideas doesn't create innovation. It's a culmination of creativity and leadership." Though you might not be able to give your employees this much time on the clock to work on side projects, you can always foster innovation through employee brainstorming sessions that allow the staff to work with new people and generate fresh ideas.

10 employee perks we love

8. Employees want open-mindedness. When your employees come to you with their ideas, you need to treat them with equal parts sensitivity and honesty. Be sensitive because, according to Hiam, the more an employee gets shot down by

an authority figure, the less likely he or she will be to make suggestions in the future. It's also important to be honest because, as that authority figure, you may know what's best for your business and what's not. You don't have to accept every idea that comes your way, but, Hiam says, "Don't just shut someone down. Say, 'Here's what I know: years ago we tried something similar. Here's what happened. Give some more thought to your idea, and come back if you think you can make it work.'"

A little enlightened self-interest: Employees want transparency. When Meddius publishes each department's quarterly goals, Gunther does it as well, not because he needs reminding, but because he believes his employees should be cognizant of where the organization's going. "Employees, especially the younger work force, want transparency," he says. While it's not necessary to publish that information, Hiam emphasizes that the communication channel between a manager and his or her employees should always be open. "That's why you need to build it by talking about ordinary everyday things," he says. "You need to have rehearsed talking about ordinary things before you can talk about anything major."

MANAGING EMPLOYEES

An effective boss builds an atmosphere of open communication

Open communication is a major factor in employee satisfaction. An employee must be able to approach and talk openly with their boss. An effective manager invites suggestions and even constructive criticism. Instead of waiting for an employee to initiate communication, they solicit feedback and discuss current problems and possible solutions. An exceptional manager cares about the employee and realizes that worker feedback is critical for the productivity of the organization.

Trust is critical to a good working relationship

Do you consider yourself to be honest and fair? Do you deliver promises when you have made them? Do you evaluate your own strengths and weaknesses as well as your employees?

The best bosses deal with their employees in the way in which they would like to be dealt with themselves. Employees' feelings about work, no matter how insignificant, should be important to management. Deal fairly with each employee, not allowing favoritism or personality difference to affect judgment. When a worker trusts their boss, they are motivated to greater productivity, achievement and loyalty.

A supportive environment motivates employees

A manager should support their employees when appropriate. The notion that we are a team and we work together creates a sense of security for employees. Workers should be openly appreciated when appropriate and constructively corrected, in private, when necessary. Problem solving is a mutual effort. A supportive boss has compassion and empathy for their employees.

A supportive boss has a genuine interest in workers as individuals

A good manager takes time to get to know each employee's personality, needs, and goals and learns something about the employee's personal life. Such bosses get the optimal performance because they are able to bring out each employee's unique abilities. The supervisor, who is able to make their people feel important and personally significant, also generates the most productivity and loyalty.

A good boss helps each employee reach their potential

Goal setting and career planning are integral in this process. As employees are encouraged, their independence and responsibilities are increased. Creativity is stimulated as opposed to demanding adherence to rules and prescribed patterns.

A good boss gives feedback

This is one of the most important aspects of an employee/manager relationship. However it comes across, feedback should be given on a regular basis. A good supervisor makes sure their people get adequate and timely feedback on what they are doing whether it is right or wrong. Managers who recognize their employees' accomplishments are usually far more effective than those who have a reputation for being tough on their employees. When negative feedback must be given, it should focus on the inappropriate behavior, not the person as an individual.

TEAM WORK

Companies hire employee team leaders to help run their organizations. Employee team leaders act as a bridge between company management and its employees. Effective team leaders monitor budgets, track operations and keep managers aware of problems. An effective employee team leader must know how to communicate and should respect all employees. One employee team leader responsibility involves keeping the team productive and satisfied. Effective leaders find ways to interact with their team, such as through meetings.

Step 1

Develop an open-door communication policy as a team leader. Effective leaders allow their employees to communicate any issues. Some of your team members may resist having discussions. As a team leader, keep the communication opportunity available. Offer different ways for your team to communicate. Employee team members can send you emails or use the telephone.

Step 2

Hold employee team meetings. The meeting should be held on a regular basis, such as every Friday. Create an agenda for your employee team. Before you create the agenda, know the issues for discussion. Bring enough copies for all employee team members. The team should concentrate on company-related issues.

Step 3

Learn the work style of each team member. Effective leaders recognize how their team members work. Some team members want someone to delegate. Other team members thrive on leading. When you have the option, match assignments to the employee's work style. Your team members can concentrate on what they like, and you get a more productive worker.

Step 4

Allow each team member to participate. Leaders make sure everyone has a voice. Do not exclude anyone. Each member must feel he is contributing to the team's goals. When a team member's contribution has a positive effect, discuss this information during the next meeting. Team employee recognition helps maintain a productive work setting.

Step 5

Give employee team members ways to communicate with each other. As a leader, explain the importance of team members communicating. Team communication helps identify work-related problems. Having a set time for employees to meet offers a solution. Busy offices can use emails to communicate throughout the work day. Your employees can send you copies of their team communication emails.

Step 6

Monitor your team's performance. If you have team members who perform poorly, you can meet with them in private. Decide upon a periodic time to measure your team's performance. For example, a well organized and productive team may need monthly monitoring. Let your team members know about chronic employee-related issues in writing.

PROMOTE FROM WITHIN

Fostering an environment that inspires and rewards personal growth, risk-taking and continual education can be good for your staff and your company. Reasons to promote from within include:

Retain valuable employees: Your most capable workers need to know they have room for career growth at your company. The opportunity for greater challenge and advancement can be as powerful a motivator as pay and benefits. Recognition that career paths exist also tends to lift general morale.

Save money: The cost of recruiting, interviewing and on boarding a newly hired employee can greatly outweigh the cost of teaching a current employee new job skills. Because current employees are already familiar with your culture, your people and your goals, they can potentially become productive sooner.

Help recruiting: When interviewees meet employees who have climbed the career ladder, they're likely to see a brighter future at your firm for themselves.

Aid transitions. Employees who move into a new position can help train their replacements, answer questions and, in a pinch, even fill in at their old jobs.

Prevent culture clashes: No matter how thoroughly you quiz interviewees, you can't be sure they won't end up as a square peg in a round hole. When you promote employees from within, you know they're already in sync with your way of doing things.

How can you nurture future leaders?

Developing a leadership program usually requires strong and steady support from the top. Given a choice between hiring someone untried who interviews well or promoting a known performer who lacks specific experience in that job, business owners often opt for the unproven stranger.

HERE ARE WAYS TO BUILD THE PROGRAM:

Educate your team. You may need to get buy-in from others on your staff who may be worried about the risk of moving someone into a job who's never done it before. While acknowledging that mistakes may occur, emphasize that you rely on them to rig a safety net while the newly promoted employee learns the ropes. If it doesn't work out, there's still the option of interviewing outsiders for the position.

Hire for the long term. When you need to bring someone new on board, consider not only whether particular candidates can do today's job, but whether they will be able to handle a bigger job in three to five years from now.

Create a talent development process. Provide access to one-on-one coaching and mentorship, along with training and development — not just in functional know-how but in people skills and leadership.

Identify candidates for promotion. Review job performance as well as ambition, team-building skills, natural leadership and other intangibles. Try to give these candidates extra responsibilities beyond the current scope of their job.

Make sure employees feel free to tell you what they want. Stay in touch both formally and informally, so employees are comfortable letting you know if they feel stifled and want more opportunities to grow.

When a job opening arises, consider internal candidates first. Before searching outside your organization, determine whether you already have the needed talent in-house. Know your state's job posting requirements, so you don't fall afoul of the law.

A smaller business with only a few employees may find it easier to adopt a promote-from-within policy. Bear in mind, though, that you will still need to invest time and resources in on-the-job training.

CHAPTER 9:
LEVERAGING YOUR
BUSINESS

1. **Focus on what matters.** Over the years, I have studied numerous organizations and have found that only about 30 percent of the typical day is spent on activities that directly create value. For example, sales representatives devote on average only one-third of their day with prospects. The remainder is allocated to administration, travel, meetings, and other less valuable activities. The same is true for almost every other "knowledge worker" in an organization. To get more done, focus on the critical tasks while eliminating, delegating, outsourcing, or automating less important activities. I have seen many individuals go from 30 percent to 50 or 60 percent with little effort using this method. While working at a major computer manufacturer many years ago, I was able to cut my 80-hour a week workload to less than 20 hours simply by using this strategy. It took only a weekend of analysis and implementation. This allowed me to focus my energies on activities that really matter, while helping others find time saving strategies.

2. **Leverage sales channels.** The ultimate goal is to maximize results with the least amount of effort. You can accomplish this through leverage: generating disproportionately large returns with a minimal investment. Let's look at selling again. Traditionally, to sell more, you identify prospects, create sales collateral, develop marketing materials, and then directly solicit potential buyers. This is a linear strategy. If you make a sale, it is one sale. To create exponential growth, consider working with businesses that already have the relationships you want to build. One partnership with the right distribution channel can lead to hundreds or thousands of sales, without any extra effort on your part. As a public speaker, I partner with bureaus and agencies. They promote me to their vast networks of clients. In exchange, I give them a percentage of my speaking fee. This allows me to focus on what I do best: write books, craft my speeches, and develop new intellectual property.

This is akin to using Groupon or LivingSocial. They bring you paying customers and you give them a slice of the action. Internet marketers have long used their affiliate marketing programs as a way of getting hundreds or thousands of virtual sales people. There are equivalents to this in most industries.

3. Leverage partners in all key processes.
The leverage concept can go way beyond sales. This is where you get the real multiplier effect. All businesses, regardless of industry have four key processes: develop products and services, generate demand (sales, marketing, and customer service), and fulfill demand (manufacturing, shipping, delivery of services), and plan and manage the enterprise (technology, human resources, finance, strategy). Determine appropriate partners for each of these processes. Many of my partners are more traditional in nature. I hire them for their unique strengths that I do not personally possess. Or I use them to outsource those areas that do not create direct and unique value for my clients. For example, I work with Web developers, an accountant, branding companies, book printers, distribution/logistics companies, etc. But none of these activities actually give me leverage. I am simply outsourcing an activity that I could do but choose not to. Therefore, I also partner with individuals and businesses that develop or deliver, as well as distribute. A training company has licensed my content and has created a workshop that they deliver and support. They spent their time and money to build the course, train the trainers, and deliver to their clients. This gives me maximum leverage. Every sale

puts money in my pocket without my having to spend any extra time.

HOW CAN YOU CREATE LEVEREAGE FOR YOUR BUSINESS?

If you are a restaurant, can you license your recipes and brand to a catering company that will do all of the work while you get a fixed fee or a percentage of their business? Can you franchise your business in a way that will not distract you from your important work? Can technology help you create a product with leverage that can scale—by creating a membership site or online distribution channel?

Get creative: Look for partners that will develop, deliver and have a vast distribution network. When their success depends on your success, you will have found a good partner with exceptional leverage for growing your business. Yes, these three strategies require you to "share the wealth" with others. But when you focus on what matters most and leverage partners for everything else, you will exponentially grow the top line of your business, with very little effort or investment. This is the ultimate key to success.

CHAPTER 10:
FAMILY BUSINESS
OPERATING RULES

CREATE A FAMILY VALUE STATEMENT

Getting married and having kids are some of the biggest events in our lives. And yet we largely slide into these significant turning points. Sure, there is a big event accompanying them – the wedding, the birth – but what's surprising is how quickly the novel and disruptive becomes the ordinary and every day. Even though you form a new family unit, you usually don't have to give it much thought beyond keeping it generally functioning from day to day. For this reason, you may never have contemplated the question of why. Why get married? Why have a family? The importance of each individual having a clear purpose is often stressed these days, but few of us will travel this life alone. We'll make our way through the world as part of a family. Thus it is not enough to know your own purpose — who you are and where you are going. You must also determine the purpose of your family unit. Why does it exist, what does it stand for, and where are you going, together?

If you've never taken the time to answer these questions, or even contemplated them, it's time to draft a family mission statement.

What Is a Family Mission Statement?

"A family mission statement is a combined, unified expression from all family members of what your family is all about — what it is you really want to do and be — and the principles you choose to govern your family life." -Stephen Covey

A mission statement is just what it sounds like – a description of an individual's, company's, or, a family's, raison d'être – its reason for existing. A family mission statement encapsulates your idea of the good life and lays out your family's purpose, goals, and standards. All members of the family have a hand in articulating these values and all agree to live them.

Companies often use mission statements to direct their decisions and operating procedures, but their utility is even greater for families. After all, instead of manufacturing widgets, you're molding children, making memories, and constructing the very best stuff out of which life is made.

Why Should You Create a Family Mission Statement?

As we talked about in our first post in this series on creating a positive family culture, loving, supportive, outstanding families don't just happen. They take a lot of intentionality.

As a man you probably have a deep desire to be a provider, and this is a role that extends far beyond the conventional definition of simply bringing home a paycheck. If we look at the etymology of the word "provide," we learn that it actually means "to look ahead, to act with foresight." In other words, being a provider means having a vision.

It's often the case that a father only finds reason to think about his family's values and what he wants his family to be like after something has gone wrong. By then it's usually too late – things have already begun to unravel, and it will take much more time and effort to right the ship.

The best time to begin creating a family culture is as early as possible (like right now!) – when things are still fine (but you want them to be even better). A family mission statement lays out a vision for your family of where you want to go together and how you want to get there. It provides a path and guideposts pointing the way ahead and illuminating the curves and bumps along the way. "Without this vision," Stephen Covey argues in The 7 Habits of Highly Effective Families, "kids can be swept along with the flow of society's values and trends. It's simply living out the scripts that have been given to you. In fact, it's really not living at all; it's being lived."

Having a shared vision – a shared sense of values and purpose – bonds parents and children together. It guides your parenting decisions and offers your children clear ideals to strive for and guidance in what choices to make. A mission statement also articulates the standards by which each member of the family can evaluate each other's behavior, and children and parents will ideally check and encourage one another as they make their way down this agreed upon path.

Yet another benefit is that a family mission statement serves to distinguish your family from others – providing its members a sense of meaning and identity and giving your children the feeling of being part of something important and special.

How to Create a Family Mission Statement

Before You Start: Understand the Process Is More Important Than the End Product

Before you start thinking about your family mission statement, decide together that you won't get hung up on whether it "sounds good" or "looks right." In reality, the end product isn't as important as the process – this task of creating your family mission statement is where the real magic happens.

During the drafting process you'll have a chance to have deep, meaningful conversations with your wife and kiddos about what's really important in life.

You'll have a chance to bond and connect as a family as you empathetically listen to each other.

As you share your vision for your family with your wife and children as well as the values and principles you think should guide the family, their confidence in you as a husband and father will increase. And vice versa, your confidence in your family will increase as you hear them share their ideas.

Simply having the discussion about values and principles as a family will guide your children to start thinking about these things in their daily lives, which, in my opinion is a big win itself.

So as you work through the steps outlined below, don't get discouraged if you think it's taking too long or isn't going exactly how you wanted. In those moments when you feel like giving up and retreating back into default mode, just focus on the process. Remember, the important thing is that you're intentionally starting a conversation on what it means for your family to live the good life. This is a life-long, multi-generational discussion. Don't get discouraged by a single bad family mission statement meeting.

1: Call a Special Family Meeting

While your role is to initiate and guide the process of drafting your family's mission statement, every member of the family should have a say and be part of its creation. So the first step in creating a family mission statement is to hold a family meeting where everyone can take part in the discussion.

Covey recommends making these meetings special occasions. Maybe you can take a family vacation and set aside a day to brainstorm a family mission statement. You don't even have to go far from home. Rent a hotel room nearby, order pizza, get everyone in their PJs, and start the discussion. The key is to make the occasion different from any other "family meeting" or night of the week.

Kate and I like to go camping at a nearby state or national park for our family mission statement pow-wows. We've been doing it at least once a year since we've been married, and I can still remember each of the conversations we had during these trips. Our most recent one was at the Ouachita National Forest in southeast Oklahoma. We spent the day hiking, but then spent the evening by the fire talking about what kind of family culture we wanted. There's something about the crackling fire and poking burning embers with your poke-stick that stirs deep thoughts.

Family Mission Statement Meeting Guidelines

To ensure a positive and productive family mission statement meeting, keep in mind the following guidelines:

Make sure everyone gets a say. As the family leader, don't let a single person monopolize the discussion. Make sure everyone has a say. Remember, where there's no involvement, there's no commitment.

Listen empathetically. Even if you think your six-year-old is just spouting off weird six-year-old-things like "Our family loves pizza!" really focus on listening to them. Kids, like any other human, want to feel like their contributions matter. If you don't have kids and it's just you and your wife doing this exercise, really pay attention to what she has to say about what she imagines the family being like. You may discover that while you're on the same page on most things, you might be in completely different books on other matters.

Write things down. Make sure someone is capturing all the ideas that get spit out during your family mission statement jam session. You'll need to review the notes when you actually sit down to write out the statement. If you have older kids who can write, elect one of them to act as scribe and write down ideas on a dry erase board or easel pad so everyone can see. If those aren't available, create a special "Family Mission Statement Journal" to capture ideas.

You don't have to do this in one sitting. The last thing you want to do is to turn creating a family mission statement into a chore that your kids find unbearable. Having a marathon mission statement meeting will do that, especially if the kids are younger. Remember, the process is the most important thing, and you don't have to crank out a completed family mission statement in one sitting! It's okay to take it slow.

If you have younger kids (4-10 years old) try to keep your meetings between 15 and 30 minutes; if they're older than 10, 30-45 minute sessions are probably best. If you have toddlers (18 months to 3 years old) you may consider waiting until they're older before they take part in the family mission statement meeting. If you want to include them, don't worry if there are interruptions, and try to explain to them what's going on in terms they can understand.

2: Ask Questions and Discuss What Your Family Is All About

Once you've got everyone gathered, it's time to start talking about what your family's mission is. As mentioned above, this is probably the most important part of the process. This is your chance to communicate with your children about your values and hear what they want their family to be like.

The easiest way to get ideas going for your mission statement is to ask questions that will foster a healthy discussion. Here are some suggested questions from The 7 Habits of Highly Effective Families to help you do that:

3: Make a List of Your Family's Core Values

After you discuss and write down answers to the questions above, generate a list of your family's values. You shouldn't create a list of values you think you "should" have. These days with so many of us having public, online identities in addition to our "real" lives, it can be hard to shake the feeling that you have an audience watching whatever you're creating. Even if you have no intention of sharing your mission statement on Facebook, you may unconsciously try to create one you think others would "like" and be impressed by. But as author and business consultant Jim Collins argues, "If you come at this whole thing as 'we should have value X' and you don't, the process will fail."

Instead of imagining what you think other people would approve of, or what you're "supposed" to value as a family, focus on those values and principles that truly resonate and inspire every member of your family. But how do you know if a value is really "core" to your family? Collins sets this standard:

4: Think of Phrases that Capture What Your Family Is All About

In addition to coming up with a list of values and principles that guide your family, Bruce Feiler, author of The Secrets of Happy Families, suggests brainstorming a list of phrases that really capture the goals and mission of your family. For example, Sean Covey's (Stephen Covey's son) family chose a line from the animated film Meet the Robinsons that captures their goal as a family: "Keep Moving Forward."

Feiler's family chose, "May your first word be adventure and your last word love," as one of their catchphrases (I really like that one).

Your phrases can come from books, movies, poems, or speeches. Or they can be catchphrases you completely make up yourselves.

As die hard Friday Night Lights fans, Kate and I picked Coach Eric Taylor's famous "Clear Eyes, Full Hearts, Can't Lose" saying as one of the McKay family's maxims. We even put that motto in vinyl lettering above the door out to the garage (a moral reminder!) so we see it when leaving the house.

5: Decide on 10 (or Fewer) Big Ideas

You've now probably amassed a giant list of values/phrases/goals/ideas that could be included in your mission statement. While it's tempting to include every good value you can think of, a huge, unwieldy, and generic list that no one can remember will be meaningless and defeat the whole purpose of the exercise. So work to whittle your master list down to 10 (or fewer) "Big Ideas" that encapsulate your family's mission.

If some of the things you listed are just two words describing the same idea, combine them. Put a star by the values/phrases/goals/ideas everyone feels sure about. Then take the concepts that you feel are important, but aren't sure if they're top 10 materials, and put them in pairs. Think about two of those values side by side, and ask your family which of the two is more important. Then eliminate the other. Keep pitting the survivors against each other until you're down to 10 or less. One effective and democratic way to hone your list was described in The 7 Habits of Highly Effective Families: "We put all the words on a big flip chart and gave everyone ten votes. They could use up to three votes per item if they wished, but they could not spend more than ten votes in total. After the vote, we were left with about ten items that were important to everyone."

6: Write Out Your Family Mission Statement

Once you have your list of Big Ideas, it's time to synthesize them into a single mission statement. Brace yourself – this can be difficult. Don't expect to crank it out in a single sitting. As you write out your mission statement, keep in mind the following guidelines: Keep it short. Mission statements work best if they're kept short, because short is memorable. If you turn your family mission statement into something that rivals Ulysses in length, it becomes utterly useless. Give yourself a low maximum word count. Writing always turns out better when you place constraints on it because it forces you to really think about what you put down. Try to keep your mission statement under 100 words. Make it collaborative. Your family might decide to delegate the writing process to you. But you can also suggest doing it collaboratively. For example, task each member of the family with writing phrases for 2-3 of your Big Ideas. Then have them present their work for family discussion and approval. Even if you do most of the writing yourself, get plenty of feedback from the other members of your family and give them a final vote of approval. There isn't one right way to write a family mission statement. Some families write out their mission statement essay style; others create a bullet point list of the values that they strive to live by. Both are fine, as well as any number of other creative formats. In The 7 Habits of Highly Effective Families, Covey mentions a few families that even wrote their mission statement as a song. That's cool. A little too Osmond-y for my tastes, but hey, to each their own.

6: Hang Your Family Mission Statement in a Prominent Place in the House

Once your family is happy with the mission statement, consider printing it up on some high falootin' fabric paper, framing it, and then hanging it up in a prominent place in the house. Now you have a constant visual reminder of what your family is all about and what you're striving for together.

7: Refer to Your Mission Statement Daily & Use It

A family mission statement is useless if you don't use it. As you go about your day-to-day life, be intentional (there's that word again!) about finding teaching moments in which you can refer back to your family mission statement.

8: Re-Draft When Appropriate

Families change as the years go by — kids get older and life-changing events occur. Feel free to adjust your mission statement when you think it's appropriate, but don't make it a frequent occurrence. It should be like amending the U.S. Constitution — rarely and with reservation.

FAMILY CODE OF CONDUCT

Conflicts are part of a normal experience for many small start-ups and family-owned businesses. But even more so when those businesses don't follow a formal management structure that encompasses standard policies and practices. Starting out, most businesses have an informal management style, says Don Schwerzler, a family business expert in Lawrenceville, Georgia. But this can actually inhibit the growth and profitability of the business—a kind of glass ceiling that keeps the family business from reaching its true potential, he says. It also impedes conflict resolution. When it comes to conflicts of interest in family businesses, Schwerzler believes these matters are more difficult to resolve, because there are three levels of interests at play—family issues, business issues, and ownership issues. "A dispute that occurs in one area can quickly cascade into the other areas." If you are involved in a family business where everyday seems like a battlefield, then you should consider outside counsel, he suggests. Seek out a mediator or consultant—family business therapists much like a marriage counselor—to help deal with family feuds, clashes about business strategy, and decisions about succession. By understanding the family dynamics, this person can act as a negotiator and devise productive resolutions. Schwerzler says that every family business is unique and complex in its own way, so boiler plate solutions don't always work. Still, there are common rules of engagement for handling employees who are related by blood or marriage. Here are seven rules to follow to help you stave off some family business blunders.

Rule No. 1 - Don't put family members on the payroll if they're not working in the company or can't make a real contribution to the business, advise SCORE small business counselors. In a start-up or family business, everybody does everything. But this is where a lot of conflicts occur. Make sure that everyone has a role and responsibilities that are spelled out and are very clear, says Jane Hilburt-Davis, president of

Cambridge-based Key Resources and co-author of Consulting to Family Businesses. Establish each person's title, job function, and compensation. And make sure that you have performance reviews for family and non-family employees alike, she adds. Moreover, think twice about offering a contract to a supplier who is a relative. Award contracts based on merit.

How to Hire Family Members

Rule No. 2 - Don't create two classes of employees—family vs. non-family. Be careful not to show family members special treatment. Be aware that, in a small or family-owned business, special favors given to family members and friends de-motivate employees and set a bad example, caution SCORE counselors. Also, you don't want non-family members to feel like a raise or promotion is out of their reach because they aren't part of the family bloodline.

Rule No. 3 - Be careful not to abuse family relationships. Meaning, don't either reward or punish someone because they are a relative with whom you have personal history, says business and tax consultant Augustus McMillan. "If others are disciplined for bad behavior, your family member must be disciplined also." At the same rate, you need to reward and praise exceptional work. "Treat any employee, including family members or friends, special if they deserve it," says McMillan, who started his career working with business clients as a bookkeeper in his mother's firm in the mid 90's before launching his own, McMillan Consulting in Baltimore.

How to Teach Your Kids to Take Over the Family Business

Rule No. 4 - Communicate honestly and openly with employees. Don't keep it a secret or hide the fact that you have relatives or friends working for you, says McMillan; otherwise when it eventually comes out, and it will, you'll appear like you were being deceitful. Also, non-family employees shouldn't feel like family members are more 'in the know' about what is happening with the business. The ability to have an effective communication with all members of the organization is critical. To foster a better climate among employees and improve continuous two-way communications consider holding company retreats in addition to family retreats. Hilburt-Davis also suggests that family members attend industry workshops or conferences. "These are a great opportunity for them to learn how to work together and to communicate better."

Rule No. 5 - Don't confuse family decisions and business decisions. SCORE counselors suggest you avoid letting family members borrow company vehicles or allowing them to ask the company's IT person to set up their home offices. It's also a bad idea to pass off personal expenses, such as family vacations, as business expenditures. These are perfect examples of meeting family needs with business resources, says Hilburt-Davis. "You don't want to do that. You have to professionalize the business. Ask yourself what you would do if this person was not a family member." For example, do all employees have access to the company car for personal use upon request?

How to Run a Family Business

Rule No. 6 - Establish healthy boundaries between family and business. This especially applies to copreneuers (husband-and-wife teams). Running a business together with your spouse is a balancing act. Agree and adhere to some kind of system, for example, some couples refuse to drive to or from work together. Others won't talk about the business after 6pm, at home on the weekends, or during family vacations. Try to get away from the business quite a bit, advises Wayne Rivers, president of The Family Business Institute in Raleigh, North Carolina. "Turn off the cell phone, leave the laptop at home, and go to the island for ten days," he says. "If you don't tend to the relationship outside of the business, you won't have a relationship."

In general, it should be a rule not work with other family members off the clock and outside of the office. McMillan says it's perfectly fine to ask someone a question about a project or client when you're at the family cookout. But ideally this should be a five minute conversation, he says. If it goes well beyond that—15 minutes or more—you may be crossing the line, because now you are infringing on someone's personal time.

Rule No. 7 - Use family councils to address family matters. Some family members will share the same values but not the same vision. One sibling may want to grow the business and keep it privately owned while another sibling may want to sell it or take it public. Hilburt-Davis says a structure that more and more family businesses are creating to help resolve these types of conflicts is a family council.

A family council comprises members who may be owners but not company employees. They meet monthly, quarterly and/or annually for the strategic planning of the business over the next year to next 10 years. The more dysfunctional the family is the smaller the group to begin with, cautions Hilburt-Davis. Ideally you want to reevaluate the council after two years, at which point you may open the membership up to other family members and the next generation.

The council does not micro manage the business but addresses family issues or concerns relative to the business. If a family member is working in the business buts needs a car this is something that the family council will address. Or if a family member needs to borrow money, the council will decide if it wants to create a fund for the purpose making family loans. It's not uncommon for family members to sacrifice income or take a pay cut to keep the business afloat during tough times. Again the council would examine how best to compensate these family members going forward.

Some family councils help establish three sets of plans: individual ones that help each member of the family determine his or her own professional goals; family plans that determine the overall goals of the family and the resources needed to achieve those objectives; and, business plans, which address such issues as ownership, management control, family involvement in the business, and long-term strategic direction of the business.

Typically one family member of the council is appointed to report to board members or shareholders. He or she would present family decisions about any type of policy procedure for the board's stamp of approval. Think ahead. If you plan to seek private investors or go public in the future, dealings with family members outside of a business environment will be questioned and scrutinized.

SIBLINGS AND COUSINS RIVALRY

Siblings: Behavioral research has shown that emotion-based sibling rivalry is the struggle to gain attention and love from parents that were missing during childhood.

The adult child's actions and behaviors are directed toward gaining approval and recognition from his or her parent. This need may continue psychologically even after the death of the parent.

Because emotion-driven sibling rivalry is rooted in problems of self-esteem, the primary solution must be built on methods that encourage the adult development and individual maturity of each of the siblings. The real problem lies between the parent and child, not between the siblings. Consequently, the solution is not working with the sibling relationship, but with the relationship between the adult-child and the parent. The second type of sibling rivalry is rooted in conflict over business styles and strategies rather than family emotions. While emotion-based rivalry is really about the child and the parent, strategy-based rivalry is really about the siblings. Frequently, such strategic conflict is driven by differences in personality concerning levels of financial risk. Strategic conflict among siblings has a very different emotional content than the rivalry for parental attention.

Solutions to strategic rivalry are difficult, but require business solutions, rather than psychological growth. Siblings need to develop their strategic planning, carry out good financial analysis and explore alternative methods for ownership as business partners. Businesses are often defeated by competitors when siblings battle emotionally against one another using the weapons of business strategy. When sibling conflict creates tensions within your family and business environment, make sure you first define the real underlying problem: Is the core of the rivalry emotional or strategic? Then take the proper course of action consistent with the real issues. If family partners in the business have achieved their own emotional maturity and are no longer dependent on parental approval to feel good about themselves, then strategic business alternatives and conflicts are much easier to resolve. Facilitated business meetings among sibling teams or cousin consortia is critical for finding a workable solution.

The development of a Family Forum, usually with the assistance of an expert in healthy family process and conflict-resolution, remains the most practical way to develop family agreement around succession planning, hiring standards for family members, stock distribution and other hot topics. Dealing directly with these issues in advance in an organized forum remains the best insurance policy against sibling or cousin rivalry disrupting the family firm. Another sensible recommendation for siblings who are in business together is to not work in the same functional area. The classic case study for this is the massive fallout between the two sons of the billion-dollar Reliance Industries, who both had undergraduate technical degrees and MBAs from top business schools. The extent of their disagreements was such that the business had to be divided in half. Other methods include having siblings not report to a parent. This divorces the emotional aspect of the business relationship. However, it also requires a strong and empowered manager to effectively manage the owner's children. If siblings, especially those who need to make consistently good decisions together in the family business, can redefine their adult relationships based on the current realities, the adult bond between siblings can truly become profound. They will rediscover that they share not only bloodlines and a stake in the family business, but a lifetime of irreplaceable experiences.

Cousins: Cousins and the world in which they grow up are vastly different from siblings and the world that shaped them. These changing conditions have a profound impact on family dynamics and on how cousins can most effectively own and run a business together.

Consider the following:

Siblings have more shared experiences than cousins do. Siblings generally grow up together in the same household and share the same set of parents. Cousins aren't subject to the kind of intimacy that brothers and sisters share. The cousins grow up in separate households and have different sets of parents.

Brothers and sisters are likely to experience that intense phenomenon known as "sibling rivalry." Patterns of behavior developed at an early age can haunt their adult relationships. As one man in business with his older brother complained, "I'm 40 and my brother is 44, but there are times when suddenly I'm 10 again and he's 14." Nevertheless, strong feelings of kinship exist between siblings and they look out for one another.

While there's less rivalry among cousins, there is also less of a sense that "we have to take care of each other." But cousins have the opportunity to enjoy friendships with each other that are unencumbered by the shared and often "loaded" childhood experiences of siblings.

While siblings may stay geographically close, work in the business together, and share similar values, cousins become more diverse. Many leave home and settle into other communities. Values and points of view diverge, influenced by the spouses that the siblings brought into the family and ultimately by the cousin's own spouses. Some cousins may join the business, but most typically make different career choices. Not everyone in the cousin group feels the passionate commitment for the business that nearly everyone in the family had in the founder and sibling stages. Some cousins may not even wish to be owners of the family business.

Diversity and loosening family ties in the cousin generation pose two major challenges: How to build shareholders' voluntary commitment to the family enterprise? and How to hold the family together?

CHANGING CONDITIONS IN THE BUSINESS

The changes that take place in the family as it moves from siblings to cousins result in changes in the family's business as well. Here are some key examples: In the sibling stage, most or all of the family members work in the business. But in the cousin generation, proportionately fewer family members are likely to be employed in the business. Many of the cousins may not have the skills needed by the business or may simply wish to pursue careers in other fields. Family members usually hold the top family business leadership positions in the sibling generation. In the cousin stage, there's a higher probability that non-family executives will rise to CEO, chairman, or other key posts. In the sibling generation, all or nearly all the family members serve on the board of directors. In the cousin generation, however, there are more family members than director slots and in many instances, the family has moved to strengthen the board by adding talented, independent directors. The family enterprise most likely began as one business. By the time the cousins arrive on the scene, it may well have evolved into a complicated portfolio of subsidiaries and independent businesses with interlocking ownership—different corporations or partnerships owned by various configurations of the family. Equal treatment of family members is often a key to success in the sibling stage. Siblings may inherit equal shares of the business, have equal pay, and have an equal voice in decisions. By the cousin stage, treating everyone the same is typically no longer realistic or viable. Compensation is more likely to be based on market rates and merit. Additionally, some cousins may inherit larger ownership positions than others. While equality may help siblings to avoid conflict, forcing equality on cousins who bring different skills and talents to the family business can lead to the very conflict that equality was suppose to avoid.

Moving to a "Cousin Collaboration"

All of the differences described above have implications for how the family is organized and for how the business is managed in the third stage. A Sibling Partnership was the center of the family organization and of business leadership and ownership in the sibling generation. Now that the family and the business are both larger and more complicated, the family must move toward a different form of teamwork and leadership. We call it the "Cousin Collaboration." We like the word "collaboration" because it has such a positive connotation. The very definition of "collaborate" is "to work together." The key to a Cousin Collaboration is that it is voluntary. Each of the individuals involved is making a conscious commitment to work together with the others toward certain agreed-upon goals.

WHO BECOMES THE NEXT SUCCESSOR; COE

Succession is the transferring of leadership to the next generation. It is a process rather than an event. While there is a time frame within which the transition will occur, the actual amount of time taken for the process is arbitrary. It will depend on you, your family and the type of family business you are in. This is a difficult process for most family businesses. The failure to face and plan for succession has been termed the "succession conspiracy" by Ivan Landsberg. He cites a number of forces that act against succession planning:

Founder

- Fear of death.

- Reluctance to let go of power and control.

- Personal loss of identity.

- Fear of losing work activity.

- Feelings of jealousy and rivalry toward successor.

Family

- Founder's spouse's reluctance to let go of role in firm.

- Norms against discussing family's future beyond lifetime of parents.

- Norms against "favoring" siblings.

- Fear of parental death.

Employees

- Reluctance to let go of personal relationship with founder.

- Fears of differentiating among key managers.

- Reluctance to establish formal controls.

Fear of change

Environmental

- Founder's colleagues and friends continue to work.

- Dependence of clients on founder.

- Cultural values that discourage succession planning.

Overcoming the forces against succession planning requires the commitment of the family and employees of the business.

Succession occurs in four phases: initiation, selection, education and transition. A discussion of each phase follows.

Initiation: The initiation phase is that period of time when the children learn about the family business. It occurs from the time the children are born. A child can receive either a positive or a negative impression of the family business. If parents bring home the negative aspects of the business, complaining about it and about employees and relatives, the children will view the business in a very poor light. Other ways to destroy children's interest in the business is to be secretive about it or to convey an unwelcome or a hands-off attitude. There are families in which children are welcome to join the family business, but no one has told them so. Owners are often cautious about systematically conditioning their children to enter the family business, an attitude that stems primarily from their awareness of individual differences and their belief that their children should be free to select a career path. If you do want your children to enter the business, or at least have that as a career alternative, there are some steps you can take to initiate them into the firm. The first step in motivating your children is to be certain that is what you want. Your lack of conviction about their involvement will be communicated to them. This may be interpreted as doubt about their ability, about the viability of the business or about the potential of the parent-child relationship to survive the strain of succession. Any of these situations can cause your child to lose interest in the business. Assuming your children know that you want them to enter the business, you should talk with them often and openly about it. Be realistic, but stress the positive aspects. Your business provides you with many positive experiences to share with your children. Your children should learn what values the business represents, what the business culture represents and where the business is headed.

Selection: Selection is the process of choosing who will be the firm's leader in the next generation. Of the entire transition process, this can be the most difficult step, especially if you must choose among a number of children. Selecting a successor may be viewed by siblings as favoring one child over the others, a perception that can be disastrous to family well-being and sibling harmony. Owners select successors on the basis of age, sex, qualifications or performance. Because of the potential for emotional upheaval, some owners avoid the issue entirely, adopting an attitude of "Let them figure it out when I'm gone."

Nevertheless, there are several solutions to this dilemma. Assuming you have more than one child who is or can become qualified for the position of president, you can select your successor based on age. For example, the oldest child becomes the successor. Unfortunately, the oldest may not be the best qualified. Placing age or sex restrictions on succession is not a good idea. Alternatively, you could have a "horse race." Let the candidates fight it out, and the "best person" wins. While this is the style in some major corporations, it is not the best option for all family businesses.

Family business owners may want to take advantage of a successor selection model developed for corporate executive succession. In this model, family members, using the strategic business plan, develop specific company objectives and goals for the future president or chief executive officer. The job description includes the requirements for the position--such as skills, experience and possibly personality attributes. For example, if a firm plans to pursue growth in the next five years, the potential successor would be required to have a thorough understanding of business valuations and financial statements, the ability to negotiate and a good relationship with local financial institutions. Designing such job descriptions provides a number of benefits. First, it removes the emotional aspect from successor selection. If necessary, the successor can acquire any special training the job description outlines. Second, it provides the business with a set of future goals and objectives that have been developed by the whole family. Finally, the founder may feel more comfortable knowing objectives are in place that will ensure a growing, healthy business. If you have an outside board of directors, you may want to solicit their input regarding successor selection.

Education: Training or educating the successor in the firm is a delicate process. Many times a parent finds it difficult to train a child to be successor. If so, an alternative trainer may be found within the firm. A successful trainer will be logical, committed to the task, credible and action oriented. These attributes, when tied into a program that is mission aligned, results oriented, reality-driven, learner centered and risk sensitive, will produce a well-trained beneficiary. All of this, of course, is easier stated than accomplished.

This system allows the successor to be placed in a useful, responsible position with well-delineated objectives. It also provides for steps of increased responsibility as goals are met and new, more rigorous goals are established. It is important that the successor enter the firm in a well-defined position. Instead of entering the company as "assistant to the president," which requires that he or she follow the president around all day, the successor (or any other child) should enter with a specific job description. In a small business this is very difficult because everyone is usually responsible for all tasks.

Nevertheless, the successor cannot be evaluated effectively if he or she is not given responsibility and authority for certain tasks. Your business will enable you to determine which criteria are necessary for good training. Usually, an owner wants to assess a successor in the following areas:

- Decision-making process.

- Leadership abilities.

- Risk orientation.

- Interpersonal skills.

- Temperament under stress.

An excellent way to assess these skills is to let the successor give his or her insight on a current problem or situation. This is not a test and should not be confrontational. Instead, solicit advice and try to determine the thinking process that is generating your successor's suggestions. For example, you may be faced with a pricing decision. Give the successor all the information needed to determine whether or not to raise prices, then sit back and listen. Ask questions when appropriate--these should be "Why?" and "What if?" After the successor is finished, say "I was considering. . . ." This way each of you can learn how the other thinks and makes decisions. It is possible that your leadership style differs from that of your successor. Your employees are used to your style. If your successor's style is very autocratic and uncaring, your company is going to experience problems. Potential successors should be introduced into your outside network (e.g., customers, bankers and business associates), something many managers neglect. This will give everyone time to get to know your successor and allow the successor to work with business associates and bankers, and to get acquainted with customers.

Transition: The actual transfer of control to the successor occurs when you retire. Research indicates that transitions are smoothest when

- They are timely.

- They are final and do not include the entrepreneur's participation in daily activities.

- The entrepreneur is publicly committed to an orderly succession plan.

- The entrepreneur has articulated and supervised the formulation of company principles regarding management accountability, policies, objectives and strategies.

The transition can be effected gradually by relinquishing more and more responsibility to the successor. One expert advises the entrepreneur to take a number of planned absences before actually relinquishing control. Let the successor see what it is like to manage the business alone. Also, this allows you to see that the business is not going to fall apart without you. Once you announce your retirement date, do not rescind it. There is no such thing as semi-retirement. By the time your children are in their 40s, they expect leadership roles in the firm. If you refuse to let go, they may leave.

Letting Go: There are many reasons why entrepreneurs cannot let go of the family business. Primary among these are financial ones. As a business owner, you may be used to a large salary and benefits, such as a car or insurance. After working hard in the business most of your life, you want your retirement years to be comfortable, not filled with financial anxieties. There are several ways to ensure your financial security after retirement. Business owners usually consider either taking what they need from the company after they retire or arranging a buy-out that will give them the needed liquidity without placing an undue financial burden on the company. If you don't sell the company and your financial security is contingent on its daily operations, you will be less likely to retire completely. Your successor needs full control, and you probably won't let that happen. Also, the company may not be able to support you and the successor and still pursue the strategy you have set for it. Finally, you may not be able to meet your financial goals from income generated by the company.

To avoid these problems, consult with a financial planner or an attorney to determine the method of transfer that is best for you. There are tax consequences to the outright sale of the business to your children. Also, an outright sale may burden the company with too much debt. Other alternatives include an installment sale or private annuity, or funding a buy-sell with insurance proceeds. To provide effectively for your retirement, seek professional assistance in this area. There are other reasons why the entrepreneur doesn't want to let go. One of the primary reasons is the fear of retirement. To understand this fear, it is necessary to appreciate the relationship between work, the meaning of life and social evaluation. For many founders, work and the business are synonymous with a meaningful life. The intense involvement the entrepreneur has with the business increases the importance of the job and his or her identity. Removal from work is like losing a part of oneself. Work is important to the entrepreneur because it provides:

- Economic returns.

- Opportunities to contribute to society.

- Status and self-respect.

- Social interaction.

- Personal identity.

- Structured time.

- Escape from loneliness and isolation.

- Personal achievement.

That's a lot to ask someone to give up. Especially important is the loss of status and social power. The leader of a firm wields a great deal of influence and enjoys public impact and public exposure. Retirement means giving up this power. Because this loss is unpleasant, it is not uncommon for a founder to give a successor the responsibility for running a firm and still try to retain power and privileges from a position on the board of directors.

The entrepreneur who successfully lets go has:

- a sound financial plan for retirement,

- activities outside the business that can provide social contact and power,

- confidence in the successor and

- a willingness to listen to outside advisors.

Board of Directors: Most small businesses do not have a board of directors, but a board can be invaluable during the succession process. A board can help management determine objectives and strategies, provide specialized expertise and even arbitrate feuds among family members. The board is usually composed of both insiders and outsiders. Although family businesses usually are operated in a very private manner, there are benefits to making outsiders board members. They come with different backgrounds and perspectives, and provide checks and balances. Outside directors don't work out well if they lack knowledge about the firm and its environment, or if they are uncommitted to board responsibilities.

If you decide to develop a board, you should be totally committed to the process. There are difficulties associated with boards (time and money) and the entrepreneur must be willing to make the board a viable entity. The first step would be to establish goals and objectives for the board. You should set these objectives before you recruit or make a commitment to any members. Boards can expand your network, provide input into the succession process, judge the successor's progress or help determine a transition date. But boards should not get overly involved in operational or day-to-day issues. The second step is recruiting. A board should have five to seven members, including three or four outsiders. Select them carefully. You can find them in civic and charitable organizations, among acquaintances and at local universities. You should know and have a good rapport with prospective members, and you should determine their ability to provide concrete advice and direction for the business. The following are a few good questions to ask:

- What is their background?

- How are they thought of in the community?

- What do your present directors think of them?

Make sure they have the qualifications to help realize the goals and objectives you have set. The remainder of the board is composed of top insiders. Your potential successor may be invited to attend the meetings, or you may choose to make him or her a member of the board.

Making Succession Work: To make succession work, you must communicate. This is the key ingredient. Use the family retreat as well as family meetings. Family meetings can educate the family in discussions about the nature of the firm, the kinds of leadership skills needed, entry and exit conditions, decision-making policies and conflict resolution procedures. Casual conversations about these issues can contribute to your formal planning later on. Family meetings do not have to be formal affairs, but they should occur regularly and have an agenda. Parents don't have to lead the meeting; have the offspring organize and conduct a portion of the meeting. Use the meetings to defuse any potential time bombs.

Anticipate problems: Will there be any problems with non-family members? If so, which ones? How will they be a problem, and what can you do (short of firing them) to handle it? Sibling rivalry is another problem to consider. Does it exist? If so, how will you resolve it?

It may not be a problem until the successor is named: Develop a code of conduct for sibling relations. This code will outline how siblings must act toward each other (i.e., in a way conducive to a healthy business), including how to work together, how to play together and how to keep spouses informed about what's going on. Anticipate problems that may arise and meet them head on.

CHAPTER 11:
IMPORTANCE OF KNOWLEDGE TO A GROWING BUSINESS

All businesses have access to an extensive pool of knowledge - whether this is their understanding of customers' needs and the business environment or the skills and experience of staff. The way a business gathers, shares and exploits this knowledge can be central to its ability to develop successfully. This doesn't just apply to huge multinational companies. Knowledge management can benefit everyone from a local newsstand to a manufacturing firm. This book explained the basic sources of knowledge available to your business, how you can best harness and exploit this information and how to create a knowledge strategy for your business.

- What is knowledge in a business?

- Basic sources of knowledge

- Exploiting your knowledge

- Make knowledge central to your business

- Sharing knowledge across your business

- Create a knowledge strategy for your business

- Using information technology to gain and manage knowledge

- What is knowledge in a business?

Using knowledge in your business isn't necessarily about thinking up clever new products and services, or devising ingenious new ways of selling them. It's much more straightforward. Useful and important knowledge already exists in your business. It can be found in:

- the experience of your employees

- the designs and processes for your goods and services

- your files of documents (whether held digitally, on paper or both)

- your plans for future activities, such as ideas for new products or services

The challenge is harnessing this knowledge in a coherent and productive way.

Existing forms of knowledge

You've probably done market research into the need for your business to exist in the first place. If nobody wanted what you're selling, you wouldn't be trading. You can tailor this market knowledge to target particular customers with specific types of product or service. Your files of documents from and about customers and suppliers hold a wealth of information which can be invaluable both in developing new products or services and improving existing ones. Your employees are likely to have skills and experience that you can use as an asset. Having staff who are knowledgeable can be invaluable in setting you apart from competitors. You should make sure that your employees' knowledge and skills are passed on to their colleagues and successors wherever possible, e.g. through brainstorming sessions, training courses and documentation. See the page in this guide: create a knowledge strategy for your business. Your understanding of what customers want, combined with your employees' know-how, can be regarded as your knowledge base. Using the knowledge in this book in the right way can help you run your business more efficiently, decrease business risks and exploit opportunities to the full. This is known as the knowledge advantage.

Basic sources of knowledge

Customer knowledge: you should know your customers' needs and what they think of you. You may be able to develop mutually beneficial knowledge sharing relationships with customers by talking to them about their future requirements, and discussing how you might be able to develop your own products or services to ensure that you meet their needs.

Employee and supplier relationships: seek the opinions of your employees and your suppliers - they'll have their own impressions of how you're performing. You can use formal surveys to gather this knowledge or ask for their views on a more informal basis.

Market knowledge: watch developments in your sector. How are your competitors performing? How much are they charging? Are there any new entrants to the market? Have any significant new products been launched?

Knowledge of the business environment: your business can be affected by numerous outside factors. Developments in politics, the economy, technology, society and the environment could all affect your business' development, so you need to keep yourself informed. You could consider setting up a team of employees to monitor and report on changes in the business world.

Professional associations and trade bodies: their publications, academic publications, government publications, reports from research bodies, trade and technical magazines.

Trade exhibitions and conferences: these can provide an easy way of finding out what your competitors are doing and to see the latest innovations in your sector.

Product research and development: scientific and technical research and development can be a vital source of knowledge that can help you create innovative new products - retaining your competitive edge.

Organizational memory: be careful not to lose the skills or experience your business has built up. You need to find formal ways of sharing your employees' knowledge about the best ways of doing things. For example, you might create procedural guidance based on your employees' best practice. See the page in this guide: create a knowledge strategy for your business.

Non-executive directors: these can be a good way for you to bring on board specialized industry experience and benefit from ready-made contracts.

Exploiting your knowledge

Consider the measurable benefits of capturing and using knowledge more effectively. The following are all possible outcomes:

An improvement in the goods or services you offer and the processes that you use to sell them. For example, identifying market trends before they happen might enable you to offer products and services to customers before your competitors. Increased customer satisfaction because you have a greater understanding of their requirements through feedback from customer communications. An increase in the quality of your suppliers, resulting from better awareness of what customers want and what your staff require. Improved staff productivity, because employees are able to benefit from colleagues' knowledge and expertise to find out the best way to get things done. They'll also feel more appreciated in a business where their ideas are listened to. Increased business efficiency, by making better use of in-house expertise. Better recruitment and staffing policies. For instance, if you've increased knowledge of what your customers are looking for, you're better able to find the right staff to serve them.

The ability to sell or license your knowledge to others: You may be able to use your knowledge and expertise in an advisory or consultancy capacity. In order to do so, though, make sure that you protect your intellectual property.

Make knowledge central to your business

In order to manage the collection and exploitation of knowledge in your business, you should try to build a culture in which knowledge is valued across your business.

One way to do this might be to offer incentives to staff who supply useful market news or suggest ways customers can be better served. You can use these knowledge management practices throughout your organization to build better processes.

As part of your knowledge management, you should also make sure that any intellectual property that your business holds is protected. This means that you have the right to stop competitors from copying it - and also allows you to profit by licensing your business' knowledge.

Protecting and exploiting your knowledge base will be more effective if you develop efficient systems for storing and retrieving information. Your files - whether stored digitally or on paper - contain knowledge that you can use to make your products, services, systems and processes better and more customer-focused.

Keep knowledge confidential. Your employment policies play a central role in this. For example, you might get staff to sign non-disclosure agreements (also known as confidentiality agreements) when they join the business as this ensures that they understand the importance of confidentiality from day one. Employment contracts can be written to reasonably limit your employees' freedom to quit and work immediately for one of your rivals (restraint of trade clauses) or set up a competing business to yours in the vicinity (restrictive covenants).

Sharing knowledge across your business

It's essential to avoid important knowledge or skills being held by only a few people, because if they leave or retire that expertise could be lost to your business. If you have efficient ways of sharing knowledge across the business, it will be more widely used and its value and effectiveness are likely to be maximized.

Knowledge sharing

Consider the best ways of sharing new ideas and information with your staff. You may already have regular meetings when you can brief employees and ask them to share ideas and best practice. You could consider holding innovation workshops or brainstorming sessions at which staff are given the freedom and encouragement to think of ways in which the business could improve. It can also be a good idea to create a knowledge bank containing useful information and instructions on how to carry out key tasks. Putting this on an intranet is ideal as it will encourage staff to post news or suggestions.

Knowledge management

Technology alone isn't the answer to sharing knowledge - it has to be managed carefully so that information is channeled properly. You may decide to appoint a senior manager as knowledge champion for your business. See the page in this guide on how to make knowledge central to your business.

Incentives and training

Remember that offering staff incentives to come up with suggestions for how the business can be improved is often an effective way of getting them to use and share knowledge. Don't forget the importance of training in spreading key knowledge, skills and best practice across your business.

Create a knowledge strategy for your business

If you want to get the most from your business' knowledge, you need to take a strategic approach to discovering, collating and sharing it. This is done via a knowledge strategy - a set of written guidelines to be applied across the business. If your strategy is to be effective, you must make sure your senior managers are committed to it and are fully aware of the benefits it can bring. Discuss with them the best ways of collecting and using knowledge. You may decide to appoint a senior manager as knowledge champion for your business. For more information see the page in this guide on how to make knowledge central to your business.

When you're drawing up the strategy you need to:

- consider how effective your business currently is at using its knowledge

- analyze your internal processes for gathering and sharing information - are there successful ways of generating ideas and do staff have a good grasp of what's happening?

- make sure that knowledge management, acquisition and distribution is a continuing process, so that it becomes central to your business' strategy

You should also identify the value of knowledge to your business. Think of ways you could exploit your knowledge for financial gain - perhaps by gaining a larger market share, developing new products, or selling or licensing your protected intellectual property to others. Ensure this fits in with your overall business plan.

Using information technology to gain and manage knowledge

Information technology offers powerful tools to help you gain and make the best use of knowledge. Some of the systems can be complex to set up and time-consuming to maintain. You need to choose systems that fit with your business and that will improve it without becoming a burden. You may find it useful to consult an IT specialist.

Types of information technology

Databases organize information so it can be easily accessed, managed and updated. For instance, you might have a database of customers containing their contact information, their orders and preferences.

A data warehouse is a central storage area you might use if you have a variety of business systems, or a range of information in different digital formats. Many businesses now use digital asset management to store, manage and retrieve information, and this can be particularly helpful if you sell online. It is, however, a complex area technically and in task management, and you may wish to seek specialist advice from an IT consultant.

Data mining is a process in which all the data you collect is sorted to determine patterns. For instance, it can tell you which products are most popular and whether one type of customer is likely to buy a particular item.

Reporting and querying tools let you create reports interpreting data in a particular way. How many of your sales have been handled by one particular employee, for instance?

Business intelligence portals are websites that bring together all sorts of potentially useful information, such as legal issues or details of new research.

The Internet and search engines: these can be a powerful source of knowledge, although be certain to check the credibility of your information source. Internet newsgroups can be specific sources of business information, but check the authors' other postings before deciding how to view their opinions and claimed facts.

An intranet is a secure internal network for the sole use of your business.

An extranet is similar to an intranet but can be extended to customers and suppliers.

Customer relationship management software helps you build up a profile of your customer database and enables you to target them through e-mail, telephone or postal marketing campaigns.

Call-centre systems enable you to serve large numbers of customers if you sell by telephone.

Website log-file analysis helps you to analyze how customers use your website so you can improve its effectiveness.

Systems to analyze and file customer letters, suggestions, emails, and call centre responses, which will enable you to spot trends, improve customer service and develop new products, services and systems.

Thank you again for downloading this book!

I hope you enjoyed this book "Passive Income: How you can create a Multi-level Empire that you can leave for your family." Finally, if you enjoyed this book, then I'd like to ask you for a favor, would you be kind enough to leave a review for this book on Amazon? It'd be greatly appreciated!

Other books by publisher that might interest you:

THE HACKING BIBLE: The Dark secrets of the hacking world: How you can become a Hacking Monster, Undetected and in the best way
http://www.amazon.com/gp/product/B014LM7 TI8?*Version*=1&*entries*=0

Social Media: How you can dominate Twitter, Facebook, Instagram and Youtube and make passive income
http://www.amazon.com/gp/product/B014WVA G7E?*Version*=1&*entries*=0

Minimalist: Step by Step guide on how you can survive on less and still live a happy life
http://www.amazon.com/gp/product/B0145FI1 Z6?*Version*=1&*entries*=0